Silent Struggle

By
Kosi Tette

Silent Struggle … is a LEEDS PRESS CORP publication. No part of this publication may be reproduced, stored in a retrieval system or transmitted in any way by any means, electronic, mechanical, photocopy, recording or otherwise without the prior permission of the author except as provided by USA copyright law. This book is designed to provide accurate and authoritative information regarding the subject matter covered. This information is given with the understanding that neither the author nor LEEDS PRESS CORP is engaged in rendering legal or professional advice. The opinions expressed by the author are not necessarily those of LEEDS PRESS CORP.

ISBN 978-####_######

DEDICATION

For my parents Komla and Sebalda Tette
whose sacrifices have made me what I am today

ACKNOWLEDGEMENT

I owe special thanks to my family, especially my sister Amadea Tette for their unwavering support and inspiration. I am also indebted to my mentor Werner Meier, my friends Abaka H. Jackson, Kofi Appiah, Yaw Ahenkorah, Ken and Kathy Kauflin, Robin Cotton, Erasmus Otoo, and my editor Kay Garret, for their candid reviews, critiques and suggestions. To friends who encouraged me to write and to all those who in many ways helped me through this literary journey, I extend my sincere gratitude.

AUTHOR'S NOTE

The following account is based on actual experiences. However, some events, character names and places have been modified in deference to the privacy of individuals and institutions. Where it has been distracting to maintain multiplicity, some illustrative characters have also been merged. As much as possible, I have preserved original thoughts and expressions to share the spirit of discovery as my personal growth unfolds from youthful innocence and immature foibles to hopeful enlightenment.

TABLE OF CONTENTS

INTRODUCTION

Although much has been said about industrious foreigners around the world, I learned after living in America, that the modern African's experience is relatively unknown. While many people blame the media, a pervasive complex also renders most African immigrants silent. For some, the reluctance to divulge details of their complicated lives has been to avoid being judged or perceived as failures. For others, it is the need to shield loved ones from their unflattering living circumstances. Though inadvertent, this culture of silence has helped perpetuate a rather false image of Africans who live abroad today.

At home, these immigrants often face unrealistic expectations and criticism when they do not return with fortunes after advancing their education, or after living abroad for many years. It is generally believed that Africa hardly benefits when able citizens reside overseas. They are considered a "brain drain," through which African talent is eroded by developed countries.

The irony is that, the "brains" that were drained out of Africa have subtly become a main source of infusing foreign capital in anemic economies desperately needing resuscitation. In some African countries, the influx of foreign money for construction of homes, creation of businesses, or benevolence to the extended family has become indispensable to their economic survival.

In America, the African immigrant elicits varying impressions. Some regard them as unwelcome intrusions on their nation's demographic balance. Others have, albeit unconsciously, been influenced by wildlife documentaries and the prevalent abject poverty of the continent's people that they are left with a narrow view about Africans. Hollywood's portrayal of Africa in "Tarzan," Eddie Murphy's "Coming to America," or "The Gods Must Be Crazy" series have not helped either. Indeed, some are so baffled by Africans succeeding in non-athletic fields, that they attribute their achievements to charity rather than earnest efforts.

Despite this, some Americans do recognize and respect these courageous African foreigners. Every immigrant knows who they are because they have been their surrogate parents, siblings, spouses, lovers, colleagues, bosses, friends, and even caregivers in times of need. They are true champions of hope because without them, many ambitious fires might be snuffed out.

Unfortunately, these seemingly larger issues tend to overshadow the lives of these immigrants. While their journeys, often from humble beginnings to relative success in these promised lands involve courage, risk, fortitude, self-deprivation, hope, and even luck; who these people really are, is still a question that remains largely unanswered.

Silent Struggle is inspired by actual experiences with the

hope that it would appeal to a wide audience and draw people closer to reality. It is intended for anyone who wishes to know how someone from a small developing country could survive in a rapidly paced and competitive environment. It is also meant for Americans who wonder why certain people risk so much to enter the United States. Perhaps it may help them appreciate their country more.

For those still in Africa, dreaming of coming to the United States, this may help prepare them better for the American experience, should they take on that challenge. For those who view the "brain drain" solely as a negative influence, perhaps they will be exposed to other extenuating circumstances that could help them understand their fellow Africans abroad. Finally, this book is for all Africans and other foreigners across the globe still pursuing their dreams. If they can catch a glimpse of themselves in this book, then they will know that they are not alone in their silent struggle.

PART I

CHAPTER ONE
An Era of Turbulence

I was on my way back to the family house after spending most of the day sightseeing. My eyes were fixed on the horizon as I rolled down the taxi's dusty window. Above the buildings and tropical vegetation, an orange sun prepared to dip into the dark blue Atlantic Ocean. The view was mesmerizing, and I wondered why Accra's skyline had never looked this captivating to me.

Not too long ago, I may have scoffed at returning home, but after ten eventful years in America, I was back. Truthfully, my life had become increasingly complicated every year since I had been away. Now at thirty, the thought of spending my life abroad filled me with trepidation. I had returned hoping to reassure myself that I had made the right decision to leave and to rekindle old ambitions, but so far, my homecoming had done little to assuage my anxiety.

I was not the only one who had changed. In the late nineties, there were few traces of the troubled country I remembered. Now there was a peculiar atmosphere of progressive peace and tranquility. Even dilapidated colonial forts and castles - once left to ruin as unpleasant reminders of imperialist rule and slave trade had become popular tourist attractions.

Barely a decade ago, Accra was a modest capital city along the West African coastline. Now it had been transformed into a bustling metropolis of commercial buildings, multi-star hotels, beach resorts, and freeways. Even with over a million residents to support, it offered amenities similar to a modern city like San Antonio, Texas.

The city's new problems were also akin to other large cities around the world. I had been looking forward to a break from the traffic nemesis I fought daily in America, but traffic in Accra was cantankerous. As the taxi driver kept honking his horn and yelling insults at other motorists for cutting him off, I broke into a wry smile. The absurdity of my expectations could not have been more apparent. City driving had become little more than a precarious survival of the meanest.

In contrast to its traffic problems, the mood in Ghana was laid back. Most things could not be hurried and people generally lived in a strange combination of peace and optimistic tolerance. Business went on even when hyperinflation and economic annihilation hovered around the corner. People went to work although their wages hardly bought their groceries. When sudden power outages interrupted evening meals, families lit candles and continued to eat without much complaint. If running water was cut, children were sent with buckets on their heads to fetch water.

On the surface, Ghanaians appeared to be natural masters of adaptation - acting as though things were better than they seemed. However, I suspected that their quiet tolerance for hardships had more to do with their desire to retreat from a tumultuous past, rather than blind optimism about the future. The irony of my thoughts bothered me. I should have been ecstatic about my country's progress; but I resented how it eclipsed the past.

Such selfish cynicism reminded me that I had been unable to shed all the guilt for leaving at the height of my country's troubles. Like the prodigal, I had traded the right to belong by seeking my future elsewhere. I could not forget that the past was why I left Ghana in the first place, or that on many occasions, I had drawn inspiration from the crisis at home to weather hard times abroad. To me, if all traces of the dark years were erased, events that had become such an integral part of my existence would lose their significance.

When I was preparing to leave in 1987, I had little reason to question my motives. Ghana was then experiencing a tide of political upheavals that left behind a generation of desperate and socially dislocated youth. After independence from the British in 1957, the new nation promised boundless potential when an aggressive process of industrial development was initiated. It seemed that prosperity would finally seep into the poor masses, but the euphoria did not last long. Trouble began in the mid-sixties after the first government was toppled. Then a succession of military coups and unprecedented power struggles plunged the country into a political quagmire.

By 1979, when it seemed things could not get any worse, political mistrust and colossal economic problems caused another violent change in government and an ominous shift in the country's destiny. For months, armed militia walked the streets and used military power to control prices in the markets.

These changes appealed to the poor, but the affluent were

not as enamored. Their assets were frozen and held by the government until they could fully account for their wealth. The same treatment was extended to those who held public office or transacted business with past governments. The resulting inquisitions led to the court martial and execution of several high-ranking leaders of former military regimes. It was a Pyrrhic Victory that left many people pondering whether all had been achieved at too high a price.

The same year, the country returned to civilian rule - but this time, economic decline became economic chaos. Traders stockpiled essential goods to exacerbate shortages and drive artificial price hikes. The banking system hovered near collapse, as wary depositors refused to save money in government banks. It was rumored that private citizens kept more money under their beds than the government had in reserves.

By the eighties, the country was back under military rule, but things were going from worse to unbearable. Widespread discontent among the masses created growing political factions with varying ideological agendas. Their subsequent attempts to seize power from the ruling government were too frequent, violent, and ultimately fruitless. Many mercenaries as well as innocent citizens lost their lives.

Coup conspirators were silenced with such military prejudice that it bred fear among people and affected the nation's global image. At the height of these insurrections, the airports were often closed while curfews and armed roadblocks were imposed for months. It was as though the storm cloud that had settled over the land was in no hurry to move on.

Mother Nature also meted out her own form of poetic justice by extending the dry seasons over several years. In 1983, drought and bush fires destroyed huge acres of farmland. Fresh farm produce became scarce, and essential goods such as rice, milk, sugar, detergent, and canned meat vanished from the markets. Even electricity and fuel were rationed, as the natural water supply to the power dam fell, and money for crude oil was diverted to import food.

The dismal conditions rippled through the country's educational system, where many schools closed their doors weeks early because inflation always outpaced forecasted fees. As general maintenance projects were suspended, students were asked to bring their own furniture. Even children barely six years old, could be seen awkwardly carrying heavy wooden chairs as they walked to school. The local universities were fully enrolled but their semesters were fraught with disruptive political demonstrations and forced closures. Graduates could not find jobs. Most could not afford basic necessities, let alone pay their own rent.

While the future looked bleak, many enterprising youth refused to give up hope. They developed ingenious ways to finance their education abroad while others left the country to work and save money. Their desperation was apparent as they attempted to stow away on freight ships headed for Europe and Asia. They dared to falsify travel documents and were deported from several countries including Nigeria, Germany, and England where many illegal Ghanaian immigrants were forced to return home. Like a broken record, confusion kept replaying itself over and over again. That was how I remembered Ghana when I left in 1987 - a nation in a state of emergency.

My reverie was interrupted when the taxi came to a final stop. As I walked leisurely to my parents' house, I still felt that I had made the right decision ten years ago even though I had not yet discovered where the future would take me. I was not due back in the States for another week, so I pushed the troubling thoughts aside and focused on enjoying my vacation.

CHAPTER TWO
Kwesi Asamane

It was 1966, barely nine years after Ghana's independence. The country was poised to go through the political chasms that would seal most Ghanaians' fate for decades. This was also the year that the young nation's first president had been overthrown. The mood in the country was somber, although young families were still realizing the benefits of freedom from the British. Ghana was still a rich country with a healthy bank balance and copious natural resources. Cocoa farmers could afford the latest model Mercedes, and educated government employees could buy automobiles from dealer showrooms. Food was plentiful and people were content with having jobs and the occasional beer or akpeteshie, the local gin, at the bar.

Evidence of the country's promising future could be seen everywhere. The tallest building, "Job 600," towered against the sky. Construction of the Akosombo dam, which promised electric power for the whole nation, had been completed. There was also the Accra-Tema motorway, the country's first concrete expressway. Ghanaians were generally proud of their country and their esteemed status in the African continent.

This wave of prosperity also brought cultural change. In the cities, dual income families were quickly replacing households with single breadwinners. Most educated women worked and helped provide a better standard of living for their families. I was born into one of these families as Kwesi Asamane, the last of six children - four boys and two girls. We lived in Kumasi, the capital of Ashanti, where my parents worked in the civil service.

My soft-spoken father was then a middle-aged draftsman. As the oldest in his family, he had started working in his teens to support his siblings after their father died. He was a self-made man who had worked his way through school. My mother was among a fortunate minority of women who had traveled abroad to study. She had a college degree from Wales and a successful teaching career. As far as I can remember, my parents always did everything in their power to provide the best for us.

Apart from the occasional truant behavior that got me a scolding or whipping, my childhood was relatively uneventful. The only incident that seemed to suggest a daring nature was an attempt to walk home from my kindergarten. At four years old, I did not understand why I had to wait for my parents to pick me up in a car while most children walked.

One day, I decided to join a group of children on their way home after school. For several minutes, I enjoyed listening to their silly jokes and conversation. It never occurred to me that these children lived closer to the school or that they had older siblings to chaperone them. Slowly but surely the group continued to shrink. Soon I was walking alone along a busy highway, tired, and completely lost. Fatigue gave way to despair and despair to tears, then downright bawling.

As I walked through the next village, other children noticed me and tried to help. "What is wrong, why are you crying, what is your name?" They asked, but I was too busy choking back tears and hiccups to respond intelligently. Concerned for my safety, they led me to their local school principal who gave me a ride home. For my distraught parents, the solution was to transfer me to Suban Primary School, located on the other side of the city so I would never try to walk again.

At Suban, I learned that bringing home good grades meant that my mother would not fill my playtime with extra lessons. It was her way of correcting performance problems if she thought any of her children needed "help" in a subject. I loved to ride my bicycle, so I did everything possible to avoid being sentenced to the hard labor of afternoon classes. Playtime became my incentive to strive for excellent grades.

Before I left Suban, my oldest sister Sena, left for the United States to continue her education. I was eight years old and too young to have any real notions about life abroad, but I knew it was a significant event because of the excitement and fanfare that went into getting Sister Sena prepared for her journey. My sister had been a gifted student, and she had completed secondary school at seventeen, a year earlier than most in her class. She was also close friends with an American Peace Corps teacher who wanted to help her further her education. She guided Sena through the process of getting admitted into College and convinced my parents by offering her home and some financial support to help Sister Sena afford her stay in America. My parents were both working at that time and they eventually agreed to the daunting task of providing her tuition. My fond memories then were of the letters Sister Sena and I exchanged.

When I was ready for high school, Ghana's educational

structure had evolved into a rigorous system of competitive filters. It took no less than six years of elementary school education to enter high school. Secondary school took another seven years before the university. Everyone had to pass entrance tests to move from one stage to the next. For secondary schools, it was the common entrance examination and for the universities, it was the advanced level examination. With insufficient schools to accommodate the burgeoning population, passing these exams was even more complicated. Cut-off grades were often so high that many deserving students were unable to continue their education.

Suban was a competitive elementary school. Teachers were pressured by parents to teach their children to pass the common entrance exam. Most parents had already selected a secondary school and were prepared to go to extreme lengths to ensure that their children made the grade. Often, these measures placed the young students under a lot of pressure.

My parents did not push me into choosing any particular school. That pressure came from my best friend who wanted to attend his father's prestigious alma mater, Oman Secondary School. Oman had one of the country's highest grade requirements and I knew that making the cut-off would not be easy. I learned to dedicate part of my playtime to studying and eventually gained the admission I needed.

Secondary school was the most important educational experience for me. It was where I developed character traits that stayed with me into my adult life. Aside from competitive academics, boarding schools such as Oman engendered discipline and social maturity. While on campus, we had to obey strict rules not too different from a military boot camp. No one was allowed outside the school boundaries without written permission.

Typical of most secondary schools in Ghana, Oman had been built during the latter part of the colonial period, when independence was popular and the British rulers were agreeable to educating native talent to run the country once it was free. The school was located on the outskirts of Kumasi, spanning about two square miles of fenced campus grounds, beautiful lawns, and flower gardens.

Gray and white dormitory blocks housed almost nine hundred students. Residential houses such as McCarthy, Dickerson, and Churchill were reminiscent of the missionary influence that helped start the school while Aggrey, Prempeh, and Osei Tutu, were named after revered Ghanaian leaders and Ashanti kings.

Classrooms and other academic buildings were only a short walk from the dormitories. We dined in a large hall conveniently sandwiched between the classrooms and the dormitories. Along with the students, the school housed most of its teachers and staff. Their bungalows were arranged strategically around the dorms so that it was almost impossible to break bounds without being spotted.

A hierarchical pyramid of authority controlled our academic and social conduct. Monitors reported to prefects who answered to the housemasters who in turn reported to the headmaster. The housemasters lived closest to the dorms, allowing the overzealous ones easy access for surprise inspections. Each dormitory had two student house prefects and several monitors to assist them. Some of these monitors were worse than the prefects themselves in the degree to which they applied wicked schemes to flaunt their power.

All campus work was the students' responsibility at Oman. First year students were the workhorses. They cut the grass, trimmed the hedges, swept the grounds and classrooms, cleaned windows, watered flowerbeds, and performed all menial tasks. Sophomores were not much better off, but they could send freshmen on errands – if they had the physical stature.

Each house had at least four large rectangular dorm rooms that housed twenty to thirty students each, on bunk beds and single beds. Sleeping arrangements followed the same pattern as work assignments. Freshmen on top of bunk beds, second year students at the bottom while the third, fourth and the few fifth year students slept on the opposite row of single beds. A responsible fourth year student was the dormitory monitor to ensure that the dorms were kept clean, the beds made up, and the lights-out protocol adhered to at all times.

On any given weekday, students woke up to the toll of the rising bell at six. Morning worship began at seven and classes fifteen minutes later. This left about an hour after rising for students to complete their chores or study before heading to the assembly hall for the mandatory morning prayers. At eight thirty, the bell tolled for breakfast releasing a flood of hungry students rushing to the dining hall with their cutlery in hand. The main class session continued until one-thirty in the afternoon punctuated by two recess breaks. The half-hour lunch culminated in a mandatory siesta for all students.

After three, students were free. Most returned to the classrooms to study, but freshmen and sophomores had to complete their evening chores before the bell tolled for dinner at six. Prep time, a mandatory study session where all students were expected to remain in the classrooms, began an hour later. Juniors' lights-out, which included students in form three and below, was at nine - leaving freshmen and sophomores a half hour after prep to scrub the bathhouses, and be physically in their beds by the toll of the bell.

At ten thirty, the night security shut off electric power to the dorms and classrooms, and all students including seniors were expected to be in their beds. Although this protocol was very strict, ambitious students found ways to study after the lights were turned out. Some set up tables and chairs under streetlights while others used kerosene lanterns to continue studying until the wee hours of the morning. Breaking the school rules to study late into the night was called "mining."

Any student of authority could use corporal punishment when their subordinates did not perform assignments satisfactorily. The dorm monitor could punish a student for being late for siesta, or the house prefect could punish the dorm monitor for failing to keep his dorm under control. These sanctioned punishments ranged from bamboo caning or belt whips, kneeling on concrete or gravel floors, cutting grass, to humiliating military drilling by the school sergeant major - a retired war veteran who trained the school's army cadets. His punishment was reserved for major offenses, such as breaking school bounds without permission or willful destruction of school property.

This ex-military man looked intimidating with his face marred with prominent tribal marks. He brooked neither challenge nor argument. Typically, his lashes left a student bruised for days, and his drills were so hard on the body that it felt like being in a ring with a heavyweight boxer. No one who experienced any of his drills would wish them on anyone but their worst enemy.

Fifth year students did practically nothing. They were deliberately assigned no duties to allow them adequate study time to prepare for the ordinary level examinations. If they made the grade, they returned for two more years to prepare for the advanced level exam. While most were too busy studying to bother their juniors, a few notorious tyrants flaunted their seniority at every opportunity.

They would send freshmen on irrational errands and punish them for talking in the dorm or for washing their clothes improperly. They would sometimes require junior students to copy notes from classes they had skipped, make their beds for them, or even fan them while they took a nap in the hot tropical afternoons. These were truly the informal kings of the school's power structure. Even prefects and housemasters sometimes had trouble keeping them under control.

The lower sixth form comprised of students who had successfully passed the ordinary level examinations with grades above the school's cut-off. Here again, the high minimum grade required for admission eliminated more than half of the fifth year graduating class. This competitive exam placed the passing students on a pedestal, making lower six more like an academic hiatus called "sweet lower."

Any responsibility the lower six students undertook was voluntary. Ambitious ones cultivated alliances with the exiting prefects in the hopes of being named their successors. This was an excellent arrangement for the upper sixth form prefects who had less than a year to prepare for the exam that determined their eligibility to enter the university.

If the ordinary level was a tempest, then the advanced level exam was an unwieldy tornado. With only three universities in the country, less than fifteen percent of the graduating class could gain admission into college. Preparation for the exam was a true test of academic discipline, studying stamina, and sheer will power - the tenets of secondary education in a boarding school.

I enrolled at Oman in September 1978, unprepared for the rigors of national exams or Oman's lopsided boarding politics. Months earlier, my parents had bought me a black metal trunk to keep my clothes and valuables, and a wooden "chop box," to store books and provisions. Boarding school food was not very nutritious, so we improvised with supplements such as canned meats, milk, sugar, and "gari," a starchy grain made from cassava tuber.

Those who could afford it also brought a fancy homemade sauce called "shitor," made from fried dried pepper and minced shrimps. Gari could be combined with water, sugar, and canned milk to make a cereal or mixed with the pepper sauce and canned meat for an improvised entree. Without access to refrigeration, the long shelf life of the inexpensive crispy gari, made it an ideal staple for boarding school.

On the first day of school, I was dropped off at Aggrey House, my assigned dormitory. The campus was bustling, as most students were eager to meet old friends and share vacation experiences. Except the sixth formers who dressed in blue shirts and khaki pants, everyone wore white shirts and khaki shorts.

It was not difficult to spot other freshmen - our clothing was usually new and a few sizes larger than our small bodies. I wore hand-me-downs from my older brothers and it showed. The faded oversized shirts and drooping shorts were dead giveaways, making me an easy target for ridicule by my classmates and seniors.

At the dining hall, the unwritten rule was "seniors first." We sat on long benches at designated tables, which accommodated eighteen students from form one to upper-six. Freshmen served, starting with the sixth formers. On the rare occasions when there was any meat, the seniors had the first selection while we watched hungrily as the portions dwindled rapidly. A fortunate form two student usually claimed the last piece. It was wishful thinking that the meat would ever make it to us. We got the dregs of everything and the food tasted horrible, but after two weeks, taste no longer mattered. I was always hungry and could not afford to forfeit any of my paltry portions.

Most seniors at Oman had intriguing nicknames. Zados, whose real name was Dotse Zormelo, was my dorm monitor. Others adopted aliases such as Scientific, Ophege, Man Apem, or Pipirrow. These eccentric aliases clued me in on each senior's personality. My assistant dorm monitor was

Obibini from Maa Ban, a small village deep in the Ashanti region. I was initially relieved that Zados had attended Suban Primary too. Maybe life would not be so bad. But Zados hardly spent any time in the dorms. He was always in the classroom studying.

Obibini, however, seldom left the dorm. He was a few years older than the average in his class and more mature, yet his opinion of city boys like me was lower than a snake's belly – he thought we were spoiled children who lacked the discipline to be in boarding school. He was our self-appointed judge, jury, and disciplinarian. Within a week, the nightmare of dorm life, once only gleaned from my brothers' anecdotes, became painfully real. I thought living under such uncompromising conditions equated to daily misery. Unless I wanted to cry every day, I needed to devise a good strategy for staying out of trouble.

A few days into the term, I was awakened at six by the toll of the rising bell. I groggily stumbled out of bed to get my bath articles from my trunk before walking downstairs to the external bathhouse. There were ten shower booths but every one of them was occupied. Still unaccustomed to the communal arrangement, I easily made my first critical mistake of the day.

My eyes got fixated on a senior student whose enormous schlong stretched close to his knees. I had never seen anything that big, and my curious stare was my undoing. It was Crazy Akoto, a notorious form-five student known to act out strangely when excessive studying had gone to his head. With dark eyes bloodshot from "mining," he screamed at me. "Hey swine! What are you looking at?" I quickly looked away and said timidly, "Nothing, senior." Akoto muttered a few expletives and demanded that I show up for punishment after classes for staring at him.

I shrugged off the incident and did not show up as

requested - my second mistake. When I arrived in the dorm that evening after prep, my mattress and pillow were gone. Akoto had come to the dorm room looking for me after I did not show up for punishment that afternoon. To ensure that I would come to see him, he seized my mattress.

I had exactly thirty minutes to receive my punishment and be back in bed or I would have to tangle with the overzealous Obibini for being absent from my bed during lights-out. That meant sleeping with an extra sore bottom from the belt lashes I was sure to receive from the assistant dorm monitor. In the short time I had known him, Obibini had never excused anyone from punishment.

When I finally reported to Akoto, he was in no mood to accept my guilty plea with the mandatory punishment; the greedy senior wanted more. He demanded a can of corned beef in exchange for my freedom. I stubbornly refused. My mother had struggled to obtain the few provisions I had brought to school. I was not about to give them to this unreasonable senior.

Such righteous stubbornness got me nowhere. Instead of giving me some lashes and allowing me to go, Akoto decided to send me all over the campus on meaningless errands. Soon, it was past juniors' lights out and I wished I had acquiesced and given him the corned beef. All my colleagues were in bed and I stood out like a sore thumb. The other seniors I met concluded that, a lone freshman that late must have done something really wrong and were too eager to mete out more punishment. After several errant knocks on the head, ridicule and additional errands, all I wanted was the comfort of my bed.

By the time Akoto was through with me, it was past ten thirty, the seniors' lights out. As expected, I came away with a very sore bottom. I tried to creep unnoticed into bed, but Obibini spotted me the minute I crawled through the door. I spent the next half-hour kneeling on the floor while Obibini made me drink a full bottle of water. The latter meant that I would be waking up several times in the night to use the bathroom, and effectively eliminated any chance of a restful sleep.

I was so humbled by the experience that I promised myself to stay out of trouble. The supreme rule of survival was strict obedience. Now I understood how minor transgressions could spiral into uncontrollable trouble. As freshmen, we had only two safe havens. Either we joined the religious scripture union for protection by a mentor, or simply did our chores while staying clear of the notorious seniors. I was not regular at scripture meetings. Without a mentor, I woke up early and completed my morning chores in the dark before the other students climbed out of bed. This gave me extra time in the classroom to prepare for my classes before the seniors woke up. Soon I developed a discipline that made dorm life bearable enough for me to focus on my academic work - which was already in jeopardy. Somehow, I needed to balance dorm life with my schoolwork before I could have any peace of mind.

Studying at Oman was no easy task. Students approached their classes with unusual aggression and competitiveness. I also found that social character often had little bearing on academic performance. Sometimes, the worst seniors were the most brilliant and vice versa. Sociopaths like Obibini and Akoto were revered for their impeccable academic records.

At Suban, I barely had to open my books after school to complete my homework. Now homework was a significantly more complicated matter. On several occasions, I found myself gazing cluelessly at homework questions in disgust because the teacher had never discussed them in class. To add to my frustration, there were students in my class who mysteriously answered every question correctly and always received perfect scores.

They were usually students from the countryside. While city boys such as myself were complaining, the village students met their academic challenges head-on. They were so adept at their work that our whines were muffled into barely audible whimpers. At Oman, there was little tolerance for students who complained about the difficult courses or anything else, for that matter.

A month into the term, I was convinced that I needed a new academic strategy. For someone used to being among the smartest in my elementary school class, I had been brushed aside into mediocrity by secondary school over achievers. I desperately wanted to join this exclusive club but had no idea how, until I consulted Sila, my enigmatic classmate.

Sila was so studious that his alias "Sila Mantse" translated loosely as, "The King of the Syllabus." He took every detail of class work very seriously and was one of the more focused and disciplined young individuals that I had ever met. To get to him, I had to get past his moody character.

When I approached him for help, Sila asked me a few science questions as though to assess my competitiveness. When I did not answer correctly, I could almost feel him mentally dismiss me as non-competitive material. He said he was busy but allowed me to use his notes provided they never left the study room. I rummaged through his bag and found written notes on every subject, with answers to the questions I had been unable to answer in class.

I made another startling observation about the physical condition of the pages. The notebooks seemed twice as thick because the paper was bloated from wear. It appeared as though they had been read and re-read until they had weakened with use. Several tattered pages had smudges and pencil marks everywhere.

How had Sila managed to wreak such havoc on his

notebooks after only four weeks of school? A covert glance at Sila answered my question. He was sitting at his desk with his head cradled in his palms. His nose was so dangerously close to the book that he could easily have been asleep. When I summoned enough courage to interrupt the guru, I was ignored for a full minute before Sila slowly turned his attention to me with a frown on his face.

"What do you want?" he asked.

"Where did you get the notes?" I responded sheepishly.

"I wrote them." Sila said; with arched eyebrows.

"Where did you get the information? I could not find it in the teachers notes." I knew I was being a pest.

"Did you read the recommended text books?" Sila asked.

"I skimmed the pages we covered in class." I said, but received no further answers from Sila who returned to his books. The gesture summarized his opinion of me and I wisely remained silent and returned to his notes.

Sila had written elaborate summaries of chapters in the text. Instead of concentrating only on class material, he had covered the chapters exhaustively using other books from the library as reference. Since many of the test questions were on areas not covered in class, he had a definite advantage. Studying at Oman required a lot more proactive initiative than I thought.

This was a turning point for me because I began to understand what was required of me. I began to spend all my available time studying, mining, and reading ahead of the class. My grades improved significantly in the next term and by the third term, I was at the top of my freshman class. I could not have been prouder or more thankful to Sila.

For the remainder of my years at Oman, my performance never dropped below the upper tenth percentile of my class; I even received a few academic awards. The most memorable was in the third year when I was among six students to pass a special board exam administered by London's Royal School of Music. What made it even more dramatic was that I had evolved into quite a radical character. Because of my academic reputation, my seniors allowed me unusual latitude. As long as I did not provoke them, they stayed out of my way.

As a third-year senior, I rarely sent juniors on errands and was quite popular among them. But I had also started hanging out with some boys who did everything from breaking school bounds to drinking the local brew and smoking cigarettes. They called me the "Mystic Man" because it seemed I could balance my studies with fun.

On the afternoon of my award, it did not surprise me when my dubious friends ordered a pot of palm wine in a misdirected effort to show their support. We did justice to the whole pot and by that evening, I had a major buzz in my head. To camouflage the smell of alcohol, I showered and munched on breath mints.

Attendance was full in the brightly lit assembly hall. The drama increased when I was the last name to be called to accept my award. The first five students, including Sila, were given the customary five-second applause. When my name was finally called, the students would not stop clapping.

The claps grew louder as I made my way down the aisle. My swaying gait - mimicking a sailor's swagger on a rolling ship - did not help. The freshmen had never witnessed such a brazen act by a form three student and they stamped their feet while chanting, "Mystic..Mystic.. Mystic Man." Energized by the palm wine, I swung my arms to the rhythm of the claps and bounced my way to the stage.

As I shook the headmaster's hand, I leaned back as far as I could, holding my breath. His firm grip lingered for a few seconds. My chest was about to explode while he scrutinized me as if looking for something wrong. If I was caught, I would be expelled. But, he found nothing amiss and let go of my hand. The students raised their applauding chants an octave higher while I swaggered back to my seat. Even the most conservative teachers broke into laughter.

After the risky incident, I became even more popular, especially with the young freshmen who idolized their favorite seniors. My peers however, thought I was unfit to hold a supervisory position because I fraternized too often with my juniors to wield any authority over them. It did not bother me at the time because I preferred to study and entertain myself.

Entertainment at Oman was primarily sports and athletic games. Although I was not an exceptional athlete, I looked forward to the annual Super Zonal Track and Field events, where all the schools in the Ashanti region competed for the zone title. Oman had a great sports tradition and we always rallied to support our athletes. We appeared to be the most disciplined students in our zone and it was one of the many times that I appreciated the collective effect of our controlled campus environment.

The games were characterized by rivalry between Oman and the Mines Technical School. Their athletes were generally older and cantankerous, though we suspected that it had something to do with the harsh environment in the gold mines where most of them worked. If Oman won, we had to flee from our disgruntled technical rivals to avoid the often-riotous post game melee. I always left the stadium several minutes early.

Outside of sports, the only sanctioned forms of entertainment were restricted to Saturdays; either movies in the assembly hall or a pop music session where a disk jockey played the hot titles. Once a year, girls from the neighboring boarding schools were invited to an afternoon funfair and dance.

Oman boys often got overwhelmed by the beautiful

young girls, and revealed pitiful insecurities that sometimes turned into dangerous acts of immaturity. Bathhouses were filled with the unfamiliar faces of students who rarely took showers. The desperate ones borrowed soap, clothes, jewelry and cologne. The daring ones borrowed their parents' cars to show off while a few others rode motor bikes at daring speeds on campus.

Most secondary school students were not old enough to drive so it was a "big" deal to show up in school with a car or motorcycle. The euphoria surrounding the event set the stage for dramatic mishaps. When I was in my third year, one of my classmates tried to rub shoulders with the wealthy students but ended up paying a high price for his foolishness.

On the day of the funfair, he borrowed his family's bakery van and drove all over campus like a child with a new toy, pushing the tiny van around sharp curves and making unnecessary U-turns at frightening speeds. His luck finally ran out when the van skidded off the road and rolled into a nearby ditch. Without the van, his father could no longer afford to send him to school. I did not see him on campus again. It was one accident that could have been avoided, and a lesson everyone in my class never forgot.

I was sixteen when I got to the fourth form. It was in the early eighties after a young military revolutionary, had sized political power in the country a second time. The country's educational system was suffering cutbacks due to the deteriorating economy. For most schools, entertainment was the first program that was cut. Oman was no different. It left us in need of an alternative, but every option was now located outside the school boundaries so we would have to break bounds to watch a movie, attend a sports event, or go dancing at the disco.

I did not dare leave campus until my fourth year when I needed relief from marathon study hours. Getting caught kept most junior students in school, but some of us devised ingenious ways to create our own fun. There were a few back-roads through bushes and ravines, allowing us to sneak off campus at night. We dressed in casual jeans and shirts to blend with the crowd outside the school.

For most of my friends, breaking school bounds had an adventurous allure. I often wondered why we even bothered since it provided only a brief period of gratification. For starters, it was very stressful. My anxiety attacks always began when we stopped in the middle of dense shrubs and ravines to change into our jeans and hide our school uniforms. The paths were infested with poisonous snakes, scorpions, and centipedes, and I was deathly scared of snakes.

Once outside the campus, we had to remain alert to avoid bumping into any of the school staff accidentally. Then there was the admission fee, which we could never really afford. Too often, we returned with our stomachs growling and wishing we had spent the money on a decent meal instead. Even if we arrived safely back to the dorms, the roll could have been called, and we could still face drilling by the cadet sergeant major or, much worse, suspension from school. Perhaps, it was this evil therapy that kept my sanity balanced, because I did not understand why I put myself through this.

It was also in form four that I learned about peer pressure and drugs. One of my closest friends was Shaibu, whose father had been a high-ranking official in the previous government. Being his father's only son, Shaibu was spoiled. His father gave him access to more money than any student needed - especially when the country's economic conditions were so bad. Although Shaibu was also intelligent, it was his winning personality that drew us together.

We became quite close study partners before I discovered my friend's Achilles' heel; Shaibu loved to smoke weed. This boy would wake up in the morning and call me to accompany him to the secluded bushes to smoke. Before long, I tried to smoke as well, but I wondered why anyone in school would smoke such a mind-altering drug. Its buzz took too long to wear off, which interfered with my study time and concentration. At a time when food was scarce, I did not need anything that made me even more ravenous.

During our fourth year, Shaibu's grades started to suffer, but the worst thing was the military coup in 1981 when Shaibu's father was placed under house arrest without visitation.

We knew his father's life was in danger, but the stress was too much for Shaibu. I watched helplessly as my friend turned to drinking more alcohol and smoking more weed than ever. He rarely attended class and insisted on my company each time he wanted to drink or smoke.

Soon, even I could not maintain my friend's demands for company. Long breaks away from studying while hanging out with Shaibu had affected my mid-term grades so I decided to distance myself. Soon after midterms, an unfortunate rumor spread around the school that Shaibu's father had passed away while in custody. The news seemed to push him off the cliff, and one afternoon, Shaibu came to me looking strangely pensive.

Again, he asked to be accompanied to the bush fields. I was on my way to the classroom but decided that it was not the best time to withdraw support from my friend. We walked quietly, somehow avoiding the rumor. After making sure we were alone, Shaibu reached into his pocket. But instead of the usual joint, he pulled out a small plastic bag of marijuana. I tried to advise Shaibu against smoking, but my friend's tears stopped me. I could only imagine what I would have done if it had been my father. I even agreed to smoke with him if it would help cheer him up.

Within minutes, we were both sedated after sharing a

cigar-size joint of weed - much more than I had ever smoked. I began to feel frightfully out of control as we crouched behind the high ravine. The vines appeared to move towards me but I felt nothing but empty air as I instinctively reached out to push them away. Oh my! What have I done? I am losing my mind! I thought.

The walk back to the dorm was even stranger. My mind lagged behind my physical motions and I felt as though I was floating on the moon in slow motion while the ground shifted under my feet. As we walked past other students, I noticed their curious stares. When I looked in the mirror, scary bloodshot eyes stared back at me.

An hour passed and the hallucinations got worse. Sometimes I thought I saw the dormitory walls move or tilt towards me. Anything stationary had found a way to move in my world. The bizarre experience was becoming more stressful by the minute. After several hours like this, I knelt by my bed and prayed to God for forgiveness. I promised never to smoke again if I was released from the drug's bondage. It took a whole day for the effects to wear off but I was grateful. The experience was a poignant reminder of my mortal limitations.

Shaibu kept on the slippery downhill slope even after we learned that the rumor about his father was false. I could not help him. I had no idea what to do with my stubborn friend who refused to listen to reason. Shaibu was later taken out of school to an asylum where he stayed even after his father was released from custody. He was eventually discharged and allowed to return home, but he was never the same. During our last visit, Shaibu could barely talk intelligently, and I almost cried. It was sad to lose a close friend with so much potential.

Later that year, the lesson I learned on stereotypes from an unlikely classmate, further shaped my character. Moose

Palla was a degenerate. At sixteen, he had been into all kinds of trouble from breaking bounds to fighting with teachers and students of authority. He was also a bully with a laundry list of problems with aggression.

When we entered Oman at twelve, Moose was barely five feet tall and he spoke with a British accent that belied his pampered upbringing. In four years, Moose Palla had transformed into an iron pumping, six-foot macho teenager. He terrified the freshmen because he looked and acted like a pit bull. His pride coupled with an aggressive nature irritated many people and led him into trouble all the time.

He was the only freshman in my class to be punished by the Cadet Sergeant Major for refusing to accept punishment from a third-year student. Even his mother stopped bringing him food in nice serving dishes because Moose would always sell them for extra pocket money. When their parents came to visit, his younger brother was served with China while Moose was given his food wrapped in a plastic bag.

Inevitably, Moose was expelled in the fourth year for assaulting a teacher. He had taken a cheat sheet into his advanced math test and was spotted by the test proctor while trying to copy from it. When Moose refused to give up the evidence tightly clasped in his fist, a scuffle ensued. The lanky proctor, not quite as fit as Moose, was determined to get the cheat sheet. Test activity stopped. Tables and chairs were knocked over, and I watched in horror as Moose bent his head and bit into the teacher's hand. The proctor's howl as he released his grip was all the distraction Moose needed to stuff the sheet into his mouth. By the time the other staff arrived, Moose had swallowed the evidence and could only be disciplined for assaulting the teacher.

After pleas from his parents, Moose was allowed on campus only as a day student to prepare for his ordinary level examinations. He was taboo the following term when he visited the dorms. Several students would not talk to him much less share their food, but I still enjoyed hearing about his daring escapades. Despite his faults, he had a great sense of humor and could draw fits of laughter from anyone.

Moose was spending a lot of time in my dorm when some valuables came up missing. Everyone, including me, suspected Moose. After a second incident two weeks later, he was banned from our dorm room, but he defiantly kept returning to me for help with his schoolwork. I did not have the heart to turn him away, though I was apprehensive.

Days later, I returned to the dorm unexpectedly to find Moose resting on my bed. My first instinct was to suspect foul play so I was baffled when he asked me if I had remembered to lock my trunk that morning. I felt my pockets, but my keys were missing. Moose held out a familiar set of keys in the air, and said, "Are these yours?" I had probably left them in the lock in my haste to get to class on time.

A gang of students was committing the thefts. Moose had seen them rummaging through my trunk and scared them off. With his reputation, he got no argument when he made them put everything back and hand over the keys. "You are the only one who treats me with decency," he said, and I understood that he would not have intervened otherwise. Later that term, Moose was vindicated when the real culprits were caught and expelled while stealing from another dorm.

I realized then that people could be so stigmatized that the good in them was overlooked. He was belligerent, but Moose was no thief. I promised myself to deal with people as fairly as I could in the future. We remained good friends even after he dropped out of school to start a business in Kumasi.

I progressed to form five where I was scheduled to take my ordinary level national examinations. It was 1983, the year that Ghana's political climate and economy were the worst. From rationed electricity and fuel to famine, the situation was grave. My sister Sena worked part time as an Avon lady in America, and sometimes she would send care packages with provisions through visiting friends. Whatever she could provide was heaven sent, but never quite enough for our large family. My parents could no longer afford to send her money for school, and I suspected she was having a really hard time in America. Since her departure, Ghana had changed so much.

At Oman, the effects of the change were equally drastic. Nightly curfews prevented even the most daring student from leaving the campus after dark. We could easily be mistaken for political dissidents and risk tangling with the patrolling militia. I remained on campus and focused on my books. The situation was so bad that Oman could no longer afford to replace or repair broken toilets. Within a year, the working toilets in my dorm went from eight to zero. It was unsanitary to use the facilities so we could only take a shower, and then walk almost a mile to remote bush fields to ease ourselves. The school campus looked dirty, as the white walls had not been painted in all the years I had been there. The classrooms were like ghost houses with gaping holes between the few panes of glass that remained in the windows.

I learned to stretch a tiny travel-size tube of toothpaste for a full term by using minute portions at a time. After squeezing, rolling, and compressing the tube, I would cut it open and scrape out any paste still left inside. Students with relatives living abroad depended on them for deodorizing bath soaps and detergents. Others had to use cheap bar soaps that suddenly appeared on the market for bathing and laundry. These crude brands were so harsh on the skin that we called them "don't-touch-me" soaps.

Most parents could no longer provide supplementary provisions so we began to depend more on the dining hall for nourishment. Sometimes, I wondered if it was worth the energy to walk to the dining hall. Breakfast was a cup of tea, coffee, or a ladle of corn meal porridge. Lunch and dinner was usually either stale gari or some dish derived from corn. After my first year, meat was never in the dishes. It was only once a week that the school provided beans with the gari - the best meal on the menu.

Best meal or not, I could not look too closely at the food because ugly black bean bugs had been cooked with the meal. An eye-full of these bugs turned my stomach and robbed my appetite, but I was not about to give up my food. I figured that the bugs were just another source of protein – as long as I did not see them.

Studying under these conditions was almost unbearable. Students constantly fell sick from malnutrition. Boils and strange skin rashes spread across the campus. There was a shortage of teachers and the school was not equipped to support the required curriculums. School terms were cut from thirteen to seven weeks, and books were scarce. I used old textbooks and for some courses, it was entirely up to me to find current texts to prepare for the national examinations.

Though our future as students did not look promising, it was our unique spirit of hope and teamwork that saved us. We organized study sessions and taught each other. We persuaded the few remaining teachers to teach after regular class hours by contributing donations from our meager allowances to pay for their time. I was amazed at how resourceful we had all become. We seemed to refuse defeat, much less, wait for the school to provide us with teachers to prepare for the exam - a strange testament to hope and Oman's intolerance for complaining.

When electric power was not available, we used kerosene lanterns to study. Although the fumes gave me headaches, I refused to relax. I learned to stay focused on studying for weeks with only a few hours of sleep every day. My strategy was to use the shotgun approach and cover as much material as possible. This way, no matter what topic was asked on the test, I would be equipped to answer.

All the hard work finally paid off when my graduating class excelled in the ordinary level exams. Once again, Oman produced the largest number of distinctions in Ashanti. Earning an academic distinction placed me above the cut-off and secured my admission to Oman for the sixth form. Half of my class was not as fortunate.

The highlight of lower six was the close friendship I developed with Mawuli, a classmate whom I had known only casually before. Mawuli was my role model. I admired and turned to him for advice. At eighteen, he had survived unthinkable hardships and still carried enormous responsibilities. He had become my inspiration in moments when I felt overwhelmed by my tasks. Next to him, I seemed like a pampered mamma's boy.

Mawuli lost his father, the family breadwinner in form two. As the eldest, he became head of his family overnight at only fourteen. His mother was a petty trader and could not bring enough money home to feed four children and pay for Mawuli's high school education. He gave up his boarding status and started attending classes as a day student to save money and allow him time for a part time job.

The only job Mawuli could find was as a bus conductor. In Ghana, the conductor, or the driver's "mate" had a job that was as unglamorous as it was dangerous. Buses were often so overcrowded that the mate had to forfeit his seat and hang precariously on the door or running board while collecting fares. It was the only way Mawuli could work and get a free ride to school.

When everyone on campus was waking up at six, Mawuli was already at work at the bus station. Sometimes his boss dropped him off in the morning for classes, but seldom on time. When classes were over, Mawuli had to make his way back to the station so that he could return to work. That left Mawuli with only the short breaks between trips at the bus station to do any studying.

He was late for several morning classes and absent altogether on many days within the term. When he showed up, he would often fall asleep in class. Sometimes his homework would not be completed or he would be unprepared in class. He became the brunt of ridicule from teachers and students. I often wondered why some people were so cruel. It was as though they had forgotten that he needed to work to pay his fees, as well as help put food on his family's table.

One teacher had a penchant for asking Mawuli questions when he knew the tired boy had been dozing the last few minutes of lecture. He would inform the class whenever he saw Mawuli working well into the night instead of studying. Other students joined in the ridicule and called him "mate."

Even so, Mawuli's quiet dignity made it difficult for anyone to tease for long. He refused to be provoked by ridicule. Though his school uniforms were worn and old, he always kept them clean, neatly starched, and ironed. Eventually, his uncanny ability to excel academically gave his detractors a lot to think about. He was the only day student to make a distinction in the ordinary level exam, and by the lower six form, no one called him "mate." By then, he knew enough about automobiles to become a skilled mechanic. Mawuli had earned the respect he so well deserved from students who had never made a single day's wages.

In the sixth form, Mawuli and I had become close study partners because his stamina and discipline behind the book was unrivaled. He taught me to chew caffeine loaded kola nuts to help me stay awake and focused. He explained the difficult topics in class and taught me how to use past exams to predict future test questions and manage my study time better. In return, I shared everything I could with him. We used my books so that Mawuli did not have to buy them. Soon, "sweet lower" was over and I was in upper six preparing for the advanced level examinations.

My final year at Oman was the most enjoyable and most academically challenging. I had finally mastered the boarding school routine. Instead of being placed in a larger communal dorm, I shared a room with another friend - Tee, the house prefect. Tee was a laid-back guy who hardly let anything - including the hundred and thirty students under his wing - stress him out. Even the Housemaster openly admitted his bafflement about how he was appointed prefect. He rarely punished the junior students harshly and was in the habit of taking blame on their behalf. Being linked to the "Mystic Man" after I had failed to qualify for any position of responsibility did not help his image.

Conditions in the country were only slightly better. At least, the curfews had been lifted and a few products such as milk and sugar had begun to trickle onto the market again. The shortage of teachers, however, was worse than before. Once again, we rallied together to help each other with study sessions and extra classes. This time, we had to go outside the school to hire popular teachers from other schools. Our days were grueling and I looked forward to Saturday nights when Tee and I could have some fun.

When we could afford it, we were in the nightclubs or at the movies. Sometimes, we ran into other students partying too. Instead of sending them back to school, Tee would convince them to buy us beer to stay. Our behavior portrayed a lack of scruples and academic ambition. But that was not entirely true. With Mawuli's help, Tee and I spent our time studying all day and through the night. We only came out to have fun when we had to clear the cobwebs from our tired minds. It made it possible for us to return to our books with renewed energy.

Even then, our penchant for hanging out with dubious characters led to our most embarrassing moment at Oman. One Saturday evening, Tee and I decided on a trip to Hi-de-Hi, the local nightclub. We arrived at mid-night when the party was in full swing and the local high life music was thumping loudly. As we found our favorite corner by the bar, we ran into our troublesome classmate - Apantan or "Jaws," as literally translated. Anyone who met Apantan for the first time could not miss his prominent jaw line.

He was a fast-talking boy with few scruples when it came to getting what he wanted. In true form, barely a minute into the conversation, he asked Tee if he could borrow the keys to our room. Jaws had convinced a girl he had just met, that he was the head prefect at Oman and from a wealthy family, to boot. I glanced at the girl and concluded from the fond look she gave Jaws that she had no clue who she was toying with. She was pretty but did not appear to have the resources to dress fashionably. Her hair was braided into pointed cones, covering her head like branches on a Christmas tree, and her mismatched clothes did her little justice.

Much to my surprise, Tee relinquished the keys so Jaws could have some privacy with his friend. I was appalled and tried to dissuade the girl, but she interrupted me. "Why don't you mind your own business," she said. I felt sorry for her but found it difficult to reconcile her rude disposition. Tee and I watched in disbelief when Jaws left the club holding hands with Miss Christmas.

It would take more than guts to smuggle a girl onto the campus. Oman was more than a mile away and the only safe entrance was a footpath through some very dense foliage we called the Borro highway. If the girl followed Jaws through the dark paths of Borro, there was still the nightly staff patrol to navigate. Boys could easily outrun the patrol, but where would she go even if she could run?

Although the campus was lifeless in the wee hours of the morning, it still housed almost nine hundred sleeping boys. Since the bathhouses were detached from the dorm rooms, it would be easy to run into any student using the facilities. Not to mention if he was found out by any of our sanctimonious classmates who would gladly give him up. I was convinced that no sensible girl would follow a boy into the lion's den.

I was wrong. Jaws did not return the keys until three, when Tee and I were too exhausted to argue. All we wanted to do was to get some sleep. Unknown to us, Jaws did not see the girl safely home. He abandoned her at the edge of the Borro highway on the pretext of needing to use the restroom. Miss Christmas took one look at Borro's dark shadows and decided to retrace her steps back to the dorm, in search of Jaws.

We were barely comfortable in our beds when we heard insistent knocks on the door, followed by a girl's voice calling for Jaws. Tee opened the door to find Miss Christmas in tears. After telling her story we felt sorry for her, especially when we learned that she lived three miles from campus. We spent the next hour searching for Jaws who had vanished.

Neither of us wanted to risk seeing her off because, it was the most dangerous time for crime. It would also have been too easy for the night patrol to pick us out while there was no activity on the campus. We decided to let her stay in the room until dawn when it was safe enough for her to find her way home. Even so, we had to be careful because some students woke up earlier than the six o'clock rising bell. The night security went off at five, so the safest strategy, we thought, was to escort her out at five fifteen.

The situation in the little room was very tense. No one felt like talking. The stress was making Miss Christmas sweat and her body odor was becoming unbearable. At five fifteen, Tee opened the door to lead her out of the dorm. I followed to make a stop at the bathhouse. But even the best plans could fail to accommodate slight details. It was Sunday morning and the religious scripture union held their prayer meeting at dawn. As the three of us exited the dorm, we walked right into a scripture group on their way to pray.

It would not have been so bad, except their leader was Togbe, the oldest and most respected student in our class. Togbe was the traditional title given to chiefs and grandfathers, so I was mortified by the look on his face. I felt as though my grandfather had caught me doing something awfully wrong. It looked bad. I was so embarrassed that I wished I could crawl into a corner and vanish. I wanted to explain and let them know that we had nothing to do with the situation and to tell them about the despicable Jaws. But the religious group barely uttered a word. I felt that I had lost the high regard these students once had for me and was immensely angry at Jaws. Even the poor girl could tell that all was not well and wisely stayed silent.

We warned Miss Christmas against following boys to the campus at night. I could not tell if she understood. Had the school staff found us out, it would have been grounds for dismissal. Jaws, however, had the good sense to stay out of sight for a week until tempers were under control.

After this incident, Tee and I temporarily lost our appetite for partying at the local club. Instead, we concentrated on preparing for the advanced level exams. We stayed away from all distractions, and invited Mawuli, who was still a day student, to live with us on campus. Being a prefect, Tee found ways to sneak an extra plate of food for Mawuli. Together we made an excellent study team.

Tee and I never regained Togbe's respect while we were at Oman. In his eyes, we were the most despicable students he had ever met. Togbe was a focused student with impeccable discipline. Tall and lanky, he was seldom seen on campus without an arm-full of books. He rarely interfered in other students' business - except for one occasion.

It was after the final mock test before the national advance level exam. Of the three subjects for which Tee and I had registered, chemistry had become our nemesis. Our instructor had abandoned the class three weeks into the term for better opportunities in Nigeria. Students such as Mawuli and Sila, who were the best in the class, were self-taught.

In contrast, Tee and I had barely completed a third of the syllabus requirements by the mock test and were banking on the three-month hiatus prior to the nationals to catch up. Unfortunately for us, our graded papers ended up with Togbe who had volunteered to distribute them. Compared to Sila and Mawuli's 93 and 97, I hovered around 21 while Tee followed closely with a whopping 20. We had "bombed" the test. When Togbe handed out the papers, he praised Mawuli for outstanding work then turned condescending eyes on Tee and I admonishing us to take our work seriously. "You must back-up," he kept saying, "you must back-up."

Only days later, Tee and I compounded the situation when we decided to treat ourselves to a night out at Hi-de-Hi. Returning from our ceremonial-drinking binge, we ran into Togbe again. We could hardly keep our balance as we tried to scale the stairs to our room. We heard footsteps behind us and turned to find Togbe returning from the classroom holding a stack of books. Does this guy ever take a break? I wondered. In our inebriated state, we could not utter an intelligent word in our defense as Togbe walked past us shaking his head. He did not know that we had excelled in the other two test subjects or understand why we went out. After the last incident, I could not look Togbe in the eye anymore.

Over the next few months, all extracurricular activities,

including discos and movie theaters, were curtailed. We had barely two months to prepare for the nationals. Pooling our resources, we enlisted help from other teachers to help solve the chemistry problem. We chewed bitter kola nuts to avoid sleep and spent all our waking hours behind the books or in study groups. We worked so well together that the three of us were well prepared when it was time to take the exam.

When it was finally over, Mawuli, Tee, and I once again emerged with decent grades. Our performance guaranteed each of us a coveted position in the local university's engineering department. Only one out of eight students who sat for the advanced level exams got into college.

I was happy with my performance, but still could not understand our intractable academic structure that eliminated so many well deserving students, including Togbe. When the results were publicly posted, I was stunned to find that he had barely survived a single course. The only subject he passed was general studies, but his grade was too low to count for much. I could not fathom how this happened to such a hard-working student.

I felt sorry for Togbe because he seemed to have done everything right. He had spent all his free time studying and never broke the school rules; even his mock exam grades were decent. What would he do next? I wondered. When we met again, Togbe looked suspiciously at me. I wanted to say something to give him hope, but could not find the right words, so we parted ways after a brief greeting. As disciplined as he was, Togbe had become another casualty of the system, or so I thought.

Reflecting on my experience at Oman, I realized that balancing academic discipline with a form of social life had been important for me. I was more tolerant and less prone to judge people on hearsay alone. Above all, I had learned to make the best out of every situation – good or bad.

By 1985, all high school graduates were required to spend a year in a national service program before entering the university. At nineteen, I was assigned to teach math in Kania Secondary School in the capital Accra. Kania was in worse shape than Oman. The country's economic conditions had affected the school so badly that only one school building had glass windows. The other classrooms were concrete-floored sheds with corrugated aluminum roofs. Open spaces between the five-foot walls and the roof left occupants at the mercy of the natural elements. Classes were often disrupted when the tropical storms hit in June.

Students had to bring their own furniture. Books were always a problem. Sometimes, even the teacher had no copy. Since it was a day school, they lacked the structure and discipline of the boarding environment. Many students were more interested in selling petty items on the streets rather than doing their homework, so assignments were rarely completed in their entirety.

Some Kania students earned more than their teachers whose salaries were now valued at a pittance after factoring hyperinflation. The seniors did things that even I would never have dared to do in boarding school. A few were bold enough to arrive in class drunk. None of these problems, however, compared to the condition of their principal.

The Principal had been nicknamed Ogogoro, after the local gin prepared illicitly from distilled sugarcane juice or palm wine. Sometimes, he came and left school in a drunken stupor. His frail hands shook all the time. It was rumored that his wife kept the payroll voucher to ensure that he could append a legible signature first thing in the morning when he was sober.

When I reported for work, I had to wake him from the couch before he sat at his desk. Times had not been kind to him, but from the numerous qualifications and awards on the wall, I knew that he had once enjoyed considerable success. He was a true casualty of the country's hard times. He seemed to have given up on everything including hope.

Even with these problems, teaching at Kania was one of my most fulfilling experiences. The teachers did not give up hope. They dedicated themselves to making a difference in the lives of their students. When students tried their best to work with the little they had, I encouraged them. At the end of the academic year, I could see great improvement in their performance. I had learned to interact with my juniors at Oman, so my class was full every day. Other teachers, who used excessive corporal punishment, were plagued with absenteeism and truancy. After the service, I wished I could have continued mentoring my promising students to see them through the nationals, but all I could do was pray for them to succeed.

I spent only one year at the University in Kumasi; a year wrought with disruptions that permanently affected the flow of the country's academics. At the same time, I began to realize that conditions in Ghana might never improve. The first semester passed quickly. I found the level of academic competition overwhelming. Some students pushed their minds beyond their limits and occasionally did crazy things such as throwing books in the library or climbing up trees and statues. These incidents of strange behavior made it necessary to have each student psychologically evaluated before clearing them to take exams.

I spent ten hours a day in back-to-back classes, then the next eight studying for the following day. These academic conditions were a little too rigorous for me. But all structure gave way to chaos the following semester when we got involved in politics. After the government announced plans to stop subsidizing our college education, we demonstrated against the new policies. Our parents could hardly afford to put even one child through college, and it was exceptionally difficult to enter the university. We naively felt entitled to the government's subsidy, which had benefited previous generations, including the officials who proposed the radical change.

The military government, however, would tolerate neither argument nor opposition and summarily closed down the school. We were ordered to vacate the premises within twenty-four hours or face revolutionary action. Historically, clashes between students and the military led to serious student casualties. I was packed and off the campus in less than three hours. The closure lasted for a month, during which time the media launched a massive propaganda campaign against the students. They called us "agents of provocation, infantile leftists, pseudo intellectuals, and revolutionary dissidents." When the school was reopened, I was still uneasy.

We returned to the campus and learned that one of our student leaders had been arrested, so we decided to demonstrate again. This time we were fighting for our comrade to be released from military incarceration. The government again closed down the university. After witnessing what had happened to us in Kumasi, the other two universities in Cape Coast and Accra decided to demonstrate too. Both institutions were closed, and their student leaders dismissed.

The way things were progressing, I believed a catharsis would occur soon, and I had no desire to stick around to witness how things would unfold. All I wanted was an education and some hope for the future, but it was becoming increasingly clear that I would have to leave the country for that. The political battles in the universities were disruptive and Ghana's economic conditions offered scant opportunities.

Unemployment was high and inflation was driving businesses into bankruptcy. Those that were still afloat had stopped hiring and trimmed their work force to the barest minimum. Even students who graduated from the university with high honors had nothing to do. Most of them still lived at home with their parents because they could not afford a place of their own. Those who found jobs, were often relegated to fields that had little to do with their qualifications. They were frustrated school teachers and office clerks.

Leaving the country was the only hope. Most of us dreamed about going to America because it seemed the only place where a hard worker had a fighting chance of success. I desperately needed a more stable environment to focus on my academic development, so in the wake of the turmoil, I made a firm decision to continue my education in America. It was the most difficult country to enter from Ghana, but I was determined to reach for the stars.

CHAPTER THREE
Komso

Komso was a term widely used in the seventies and eighties among students who aspired to further their education abroad. It was an informal approach that included identifying prospective institutions, applying for admission and financial aid, securing travel visas, and even financing the trip.

When I became serious about leaving, there were no official methods that provided information on studying overseas. Most parents discouraged the idea because the chances of admission were slim, and they feared it would be a waste of time and resources. Though their fears were not unfounded, those who managed to get through seemed to earn their family's respect and support. As living conditions grew worse, Komso became the answer to the prayers of many desperate youth – including me.

The successful ones left Komso portfolios that were as valuable as their textbooks. These documents were the road maps we used to navigate the convoluted path of leaving the country. Success depended on a combination of academic, financial, athletic, extra-curricular abilities, and immutable hope. High achievement in any of these categories increased the chances of traveling abroad to study.

In rare instances, a student would be a high academic achiever, talented in sports, and have the money to finance their education abroad. Most candidates were high academic achievers with no athletic ability or financial backing. The most inspirational stories came from those who had little more than courage and determination. Their successes gave other students hope.

Komso was a huge gamble. For every successful student, there were too many examples of others who had tried for several years and failed each time. As Komso aspirants, we had to develop an unfaltering belief in success and depend on faith to guide us through repeated disappointments. At Oman, there was an insatiable hunger for information about journeying alumni. Everyone knew who had left the country, where they had gone, and what they had done with themselves over the years. Some of the least likely candidates became the most successful. Komso's invisible hand of hope propelled all to make the best of themselves and become established in many disciplines abroad. Even the mean spirited Akoto had become a pharmacist in Los Angeles, and Obibini was studying law at Oxford.

Komso portfolios were helpful, but they provided little information about how the successful ones actually became doctors and engineers. It was assumed that becoming a professional was relatively easy, if not an automatic transition. To many of us, the biggest obstacle was leaving Ghana. Our myopic visions prevented us from appreciating the magnitude of what we were about to undertake. Perhaps, this ignorance was a blessing. Getting out of Ghana was difficult enough. It would have been too much of a mental stretch to comprehend the stresses of becoming professionals in a foreign land as well.

The first stage involved learning everything about the country of choice. It meant going to the library to read and asking anyone who had information about life outside Ghana. The United States Information Services featured re-runs of popular news shows such as 60 Minutes and Nightline. This was how I developed my first in-depth impressions of the United States. News about the lifestyles of famous people confirmed the promise of success and increased my obsession with America.

I knew no one who would give me a Komso portfolio so my path to enlightenment was bumpy. With little information about international student programs, I had to make random selections from all the colleges in America. It was like picking winning lottery numbers. The odds did not improve much by applying to many schools; it eroded the quality of my applications and backfired.

Admission into college was possible if my academics were strong and my test scores were high. But to obtain financial assistance, my test scores needed to be in the top ten percentiles. I wrote to my Sister Sena and she graciously helped me by paying for the SAT. I applied to ten schools but gave up when all ten had policies preventing financial aid awards to foreign students. My parents were now retired, and their meager pensions had been almost obliterated by inflation. I was going nowhere without a scholarship.

While I waited for the universities to be reopened, I redoubled my efforts to leave the country, but I was initially unsuccessful in obtaining any financial assistance. Even though some schools had admitted me, it seemed I had applied to institutions where scholarship applicants were just as good. I felt my approach was flawed, yet I was not sure what I was doing wrong.

During the second university closure, I visited Kania Secondary School, where I had completed my national service. I did not know it would lead to a chance encounter that would transform my life dramatically. One afternoon, I was standing outside the campus talking with some Kania staff members when I heard someone call out "Mystic Man" from a distance. I turned to see a familiar face and a hand waving at me.

I could not believe my eyes. It was Togbe in fashionable sunglasses, carrying a slim business folder under his arm. I could tell from the red dust on his pant legs that he had been walking long distances along Accra's dry city roads. The dramatic change in my conservative classmate left me speechless. Togbe was upbeat and full of smiles; something I had never seen him do before. This time, I was the one who had the curious look.

After the usual small talk, Togbe asked if I had considered traveling out of the country. My answer revealed my myopic conviction that it was impossible to obtain any financial aid as a foreign applicant. "No, that's where you are wrong," said Togbe, capturing my undivided attention. He opened his folder and showed me letters of admission to two institutions that had awarded him full academic and residential scholarships.

How did Togbe, who barely passed a single course in the advanced levels, manage to achieve what "The Mystic Man" could not? I set my pride aside and sought his help immediately. But all Togbe offered that day was his business card and an invitation to his house for further consultation.

Finding Togbe at home was not easy. When I arrived at his house the next day, he was not there, and I was not the only one who sought his advice. Three other Komso aspirants had asked for him while I waited. Rather than being discouraged by Togbe's elusiveness, my interest piqued. Why was Togbe in such high demand? Three additional trips later, I met Togbe at home, and the two hours spent with him proved that my patience was not in vain.

If I ever wondered what Togbe had done after the advanced level, the answer stared at me in the face. This Komso guru blew holes in my application package. I was not presenting myself competitively and my choice of schools was all wrong. I was not used to believing that my work was inadequate, but this time, Togbe had crucial information I needed.

He selected four schools and assured me that, if I followed his method, I would definitely get aid from at least one. He threw out all my letters and gave me a set of sample letters to use as learning templates. The letters tended to portray an aggressive, creative, and academically strong candidate. Why had I not thought to promote my music and extra-curricular activities? I had assumed that my grades were enough.

Re-application was a major undertaking - four schools were a bit much, considering the work to be done to comply with Togbe's standards. Transcripts had to be revised to show equivalencies to the American grading system. The SAT had to be rewritten because Togbe felt my grades needed to be even higher to improve my chances of getting a scholarship as a foreigner. He emphasized the importance of professionalism and that I would be competing with students worldwide, including those with money to afford their education.

Within three months of our meeting, I had retaken the SATs and scored in the top five -percentiles. I was on a mission. I had my recommendations restructured by offering my former instructors more information about my goals. My statement of purpose was more comprehensive and meaningful. My Sister Sena came to my aid again and paid for the application fees for the four colleges. Local errands and postage wiped out most of my savings, but I knew I was onto something.

Togbe's method of answering each question as though my life depended on it forced me to do some real soul searching. What had begun as an attempt to leave the country had turned into an important lesson in self-discovery. When the admission and financial aid awards arrived, I did not qualify for a full award, but two schools had given me some aid. Following Togbe's advice, I did not give up. I continued to communicate with the institutions but discovered that additional aid could not be awarded on academic merit alone; they were need-based scholarships and loans reserved for American citizens and permanent residents.

The best deal was from Bacchus College, in Illinois, but it had an annual tuition balance of $4000, and a stipulation requiring the recipient to maintain no less than a 3.30 GPA to keep the award. I was too preoccupied with getting to America to be phased by the money and high academic requirement. Assuming I could work to pay off the money while going to school, I accepted the offer and looked for a local sponsor to assist with the balance.

I was now at the stage where most applicants fell short. Times were desperate, and some parents mortgaged their homes and pawned their jewelry to send their children abroad. Even Togbe had to work feverishly to raise money for his airline ticket. Before leaving, Togbe introduced me to Nii Ocansey, a wealthy farmer and self-proclaimed benefactor. Mr. Ocansey had lived in America before, but returned to Ghana hastily for undisclosed reasons. I suspected that he might have had problems with the law because he was apprehensive about discussing why he left America.

Mr. Ocansey's plan appeared to be simple – at least on the surface. He was offering to loan the funds with interest, but he refused to release any funds until the student made it safely abroad. He also demanded a deposit before his bank statements could be used as proof of financial sponsorship. The hundred-dollar fee was steep considering his clients were mostly unemployed students like me. For all his altruistic claims, he was just another opportunistic loan shark.

Bacchus College, however, required full payment before releasing the I-20 immigration forms I needed to apply for an American visa. Without Mr. Ocansey's help, I worried about how I would satisfy the college's conditions of sponsorship. I convinced Mr. Ocansey to write a letter to the school asking for the forms as additional proof of my admittance before releasing any funds to them. In return, Mr. Ocansey increased my deposit by twenty dollars.

By now, my unwavering commitment was taking its toll. I had shed a few pounds as I had less to spend on food. It took all my savings to pay Mr. Ocansey. I sold everything from my wristwatch to my scientific calculator to raise the funds. All I had left was my bicycle. I realized then that the implications of failure had increased exponentially. So much time, effort, and money had been invested, but there was absolutely no guarantee that I would be given a visa. The approval rate for an American visa was very low.

Fortunately, my gamble began to pay off. I received the immigration forms a month after Mr. Ocansey sent his letter. The local U.S. consulate, however, needed another certified bank statement to cover four years of college. I had to ask Mr. Ocansey for help again. He wanted fifty dollars for an additional bank statement. I sold my bicycle to pay the greedy philanthropist.

Now, it was time to apply for the visa. A limited number of interviews were allowed each week, so applicants had to queue at the embassy over the weekend to secure an interview with the consular. I was too exhausted to sleep at the embassy for three nights, so I paid a contractor to hold my place. It wiped out the rest my money.

On Monday morning, I was seventh in line when I arrived at the consulate. A fifteen-foot solid concrete and steel black fence surrounded the immaculate two-story white building. The US Embassy's heavily guarded gates left no doubt that serious business was conducted there. To us, the building was a black and white concrete enigma that held the key to our dreams.

Going through the entry process, I discovered that I had forgotten to bring my passport photographs. I pleaded with the guard to allow me re-entry and rushed to find a taxi to take me downtown Accra to a photo studio. They told me that it would take an hour to get the photos developed. With every passing minute, the chances of losing my seat at the embassy increased. I held my rosaries firmly and kept praying.

Luckily, the empathetic proprietors expedited the photographs. In fifteen minutes, they produced four wet prints on a plastic tablet, which I could peel off after they dried. I thanked them and hailed another taxi back to the embassy. With adrenaline pumping, I felt a rekindled sense of hope and adventure. The embassy guard let me in with no fuss, and I felt as though someone upstairs was finally looking my way.

After losing my position, I was bumped far enough down the queue to observe others make gross errors during their interviews. The balding consular on duty that day had a reputation for denying visas to most of his young applicants; they called him "Kojak." He sat in an office behind thick bulletproof Plexiglas windows and summoned applicants through a microphone. We sat on benches like pews in a church, waiting to be called to the interview window.

The atmosphere in the waiting room was tense. Even the

usually talkative Ghanaians were quiet. I watched in dismay as applicant after applicant was denied a visa; others were asked to supply further information. A gentleman who needed a unique surgical procedure available only in America, could not convince Kojak that he had enough money to pay for the operation. All his documents, including his passport, were confiscated until he could provide a sponsor. I could tell from the defeated look on the man's face that his sponsor probably did not exist. He almost collapsed in the hall and had to be helped out. Another woman forgot all rules of decorum and cursed the oblivious Kojak when she was rejected. She was also escorted out.

The businessmen and women, who thought they had saved loads of American dollars, quickly found out that it was not enough to assure entry visas for their children. Kojak asked them all: "How can you prove that if I let you go you will return to Ghana." It was a loaded question that had no absolute answer. Nobody could prove that they would return. After watching the proceedings, I rethought my responses and braced myself to answer even the remotest of questions.

When I was finally summoned to the window, Kojak asked for documentation showing a legitimate intent to further my education in America. Kojak did not smile; he sounded rather frustrated and impatient. Though it was cool in the air-conditioned room, I could feel my sweaty palms as I searched for the papers. As I went to pull them out, Kojak asked for the bag and all its contents. I wondered if I had left any information about the precarious agreements I had made with Mr. Ocansey in the bag, but it was too late to worry. I left it to providence.

Kojak combed through every document and asked detailed questions about each letter and my relationship with their authors. The depth of the questions was surprising. I was unexpectedly questioned about Bacchus, and enrollment statistics. Luckily, Togbe had taught me to be thorough.

After ten grueling minutes, the questions ended abruptly. Kojak stuffed the documents back into the bag and told me to wait. I hoped for the best. At least, my documents had been returned to me. I could not believe my luck when the office clerk said I could pick up my visa in a couple of hours. I was the first applicant under forty to receive a visa from Kojak that day. The other applicants clapped to acknowledge my victory. Some hope had been restored to the younger applicants.

That afternoon, I felt as though I had won the lottery. I stood outside the embassy staring at my visa. "Valid for multiple application for entry until 1992," it said. I could enter the United States for the next five years, if I remained in good standing at my school. Hard work and faith had finally paid off. On my way home, I gave away all but my transportation money to the crippled beggars I met along the city streets to share my joy. When I broke the news to my family, there was instant jubilation. Someone had finally made it.

Financing the plane ticket to Illinois now loomed ahead. My parents mortgaged their house to raise the money for the ticket. It hurt me to watch my retired mother go begging on my behalf. My one-way ticket cost fifteen hundred dollars. That was six hundred thousand cedis. I had never seen that much money and watched with a knot in my stomach as the ticket agent counted the money into the register.

Now I had to think seriously about what I would do when I got to Illinois. My mentor, Togbe had left a couple months earlier. My main concern was coming up with a contingency plan in case Mr. Ocansey's shaky deal did not materialize. What would happen to me if the so-called philanthropist reneged on the deal? Could I really work and go to school? How would I find employment when I had heard foreigners could not work without the necessary permits?

Mr. Ocansey's only response to my success was, "Write me when you get there, and I'll take care of everything." I was not prepared for such a simple answer, but I was powerless to do much about my fate. As the day of departure drew closer, it brought a growing sense of anxiety and uncertainty.

My father gave me his navy blue suit since I did not own one. Mawuli, Moose and a few friends joined my family at the airport to see me off. I managed to avoid getting emotional until I went through the last checkpoint where they could not follow. I choked back tears as I waved to my parents and friends. When I saw the pride in their eyes, I realized the impact of the responsibility I had undertaken.

With the uncertainties ahead, I wondered if all that admiration was misplaced. I hoped I had not taken on more than I could handle. My fate was sealed, and I could not quit now. I wiped the tears from my face, then smiled and waved as my friends chanted "Mystic... Mystic...Mystic Man," a poignant reminder of the life I was leaving behind.

As the plane took off, the feelings of pride were replaced with a curious loneliness. For the first time in my life, I had chosen a path that could not be reversed easily. I thought about my mother, wondering when I would see her again. Again, tears filled my eyes at not knowing how long I would be away from my family. I tried to shrug off the disheartening feelings because nothing could be done to change my fate. Too much was at stake now, not to mention the expense of a return ticket. My parents had given me five hundred dollars - it was all the money they had saved.

The plane landed at Chicago's O'Hare, America's busiest airport. Comparatively, Ghana's Kotoka airport was tiny and unsophisticated. My worries about the immigration process were unfounded and soon I was walking through the airport admiring its bustling activity and unfamiliar digital screens.

My first hiccup occurred when I tried to use the pay phones to call Bacchus College. The phone had many new terms - collect, station-to-station, and person-to-person – it took me a second to realize that I was talking to an answering machine and fumbled on each try, losing my money in the process. A kind airline agent who witnessed my obvious frustrations offered to help. I must have looked very foreign in my unfamiliar clothes and uneven hair.

It was Labor Day weekend and the offices were closed. So I purchased a ticket to Mossfield, the closest airport to Bacchus College. For one whose first flight was in a Boeing 747 jumbo jet, the next leg in the twin propeller charter was scary. The small plane chattered and groaned under the passengers' weight and force of the winds. All I could do was to grip my rosary and pray through the forty-minute flight.

At Mossfield airport, I realized that I was almost alone. All the other passengers had left in a hurry. It was almost eleven and the tiny airport was dark and quiet. There was no visible taxi service as I had expected. Only a heavy-set, bearded man in a wheelchair talking on the phone next to me. I had no idea what to do, so I waited patiently for the man to finish his phone call.

He introduced himself as Charley. Even though he was a paraplegic, he had an upbeat attitude - how different from the handicapped beggars in Accra. The man was actually helping me between jokes about the school not keeping track of its students. He said, "These guys are all gone, they probably heard you were coming and decided to stay at home just to avoid you." I was slow at catching the sarcastic punch line; I panicked at being stranded at the airport.

Charley then said "Say, if you could hold on a minute, I'll get you there myself. There aren't any cabs around here this time of the night." I did not know what to say. Here I was, imposing on a paraplegic for a ride. Charley smiled at my perplexed expression and quickly said, "Hey, I have a custom-made car, I can drive." I liked Charley's bearded smile and could not refuse help from this man who seemed really earnest.

We made an unlikely pair - an African and a Caucasian paraplegic, together in a deserted parking lot – but I was grateful for the assistance. Charley stopped by a triple black Golf GTI with black leather seats. It had an automated ramp to help him enter the through the rear hatch.

Everything about Charley confirmed my visions of America. I looked up into the dark sky and thought, I really am in the USA. Then I watched the motorized ramp lock the wheels on the chair and pull Charley slowly into the rear of the car. With the help of handlebars, he lifted himself from the wheelchair into the driver's seat. At the touch of a couple buttons, the hatch closed, and the doors unlocked for me to enter from the passenger side and listen to cool jazz tunes from the car's stereo.

Charley drove effortlessly. All the controls were accessible by hand levers. He showed me a set of stoplights that he could beat at 38-mph. He hit five green lights in a row and soon, I was laughing along with Charley, who was a true comedian. He told me that he had not always been a paraplegic. He had been run over by a semi-truck that left him paralyzed from the waist down. His legs had to be amputated to save his life. My heart was full of sympathy for him.

When we finally arrived at my dorm, I removed my suitcase and stood by the pavement to wave Charley good-bye. I was euphoric to have finally arrived in America's heartland under such unusual circumstances. Starring at the disappearing car, I felt more confident than ever that I could succeed. If Charley could make an honorable life for himself, then surely, I would have only myself to blame if I failed in America. I felt my destiny was sealed - I had a purpose for being in this country.

PART II

CHAPTER FOUR
Campus Life in Illinois

At the time of my enrollment, Bacchus was a small religious institution with a predominant Caucasian student body. It was an affluent private school that attracted students who wanted a quality education without the alienation of a large institution. It's quiet setting, was in a small industrial town along the Mississippi River, and the campus was immaculately kept with sidewalks connecting old traditional brick buildings scattered over a two city blocks.

Students living in the dorms walked a half-mile down campus for lectures and to access the library and administration buildings. Being a college town, many surrounding houses had been acquired by the school for additional housing. They were more expensive, but ideal for students who wanted more privacy.

I had been assigned to an up-campus dormitory. My

roommate Chuck, a bearded, 6 foot, 300-pound varsity wrestler, resembled a sumo wrestler. Coming from a small town, he was apprehensive about sharing a room with an African. Initially, he had tried everything to get reassigned. Fortunately, he was a teddy bear at heart, and his genuine curiosity about Africa was comforting.

Chuck wanted to know about houses we lived in, the food we ate, the schools we attended - and if there was a McDonalds in Ghana. As time went by, I marveled at how much information he had absorbed about Ghana; he even checked out some books on Africa. Such efforts convinced me that he was sincere. Our constant interaction grew into a friendship that helped us get along.

Chuck's problem was over-indulging in beer and weed or pot, as he called it. Thankfully, I had purged myself of any curiosity about drugs at Oman. It kept me out of trouble because Chuck always had beer in his little refrigerator and a constant supply of pot, which he smoked from a fancy three-foot "bong" water pipe. All I needed to remember was my friend Shaibu to graciously refuse each time Chuck offered to share his pot.

Most of Chuck's friends wanted little to do with me, and barely said "hello." There seemed to be an unspoken rule: "If you stay out of my way, I'll stay out of yours." In time, I was able to interact with only a handful of Caucasian students outside of class. It made me seek out the few African Americans and even fewer Africans on campus.

There were less than fifteen African students on campus, including one other Ghanaian who I considered too British. She had lived in England for so long that every other sentence she uttered had something to do with London. The other Africans were from the east to southern part of the continent. There were two Namibians, Hafeni and Sheya, who were on scholarship from their government, and a few Kenyans.

Hafeni and Sheya were extremely smart, but also wild. They stayed glued to their phone and always invited me when they had an extra bottle of beer. Sheya missed his fiancée so much that he was accumulating huge phone bills, just staying in touch. Hafeni's phone calls to his family and buddies back home in Windhoek were to blame for his big bills.

The most intriguing aspect about them was their uncompromising intolerance for racial prejudice. Though I had little interest in politics, I respected their convictions and desire to return home after their education to make a difference. Their latent anger was understandable because, in 1987, Namibia was still under Apartheid South African rule; they were still struggling for the same privileges that Ghana had enjoyed for three decades.

I learned about their difficult experiences under Apartheid and realized that many Namibians had lost their lives or had fled their country as refugees. Many of their friends in America were Namibian political exiles. I empathized with them because - much as I was also running from hardships - my situation seemed less profound. Ghanaians were responsible for their unstable political system and economic mistakes, not generations of colonialists.

The Kenyans were very studious and assimilated much easier. Their British colonial influence was like Ghana's, and I discovered startling similarities between our respective educational systems, cultures, norms, and popular commercial products such as detergents and cereals. I thought it was unfortunate that I had to leave my own country to realize how similar we were.

The African American population was much larger, though still a minority on campus. Most students were from Chicago - their expensive cars suggested they were from upwardly mobile homes. Through a well-organized Black Students Union, they included all the Africans in their activities. Nevertheless, some treated me no differently than Chuck's friends. I was sometimes ignored when I reached out to them. I feared they considered me as an unwelcome reminder of another generation of Africans who had sold their ancestors into slavery; I had no idea how to handle their resentment.

I understood that, like Chuck, their view of Africa had been influenced by movies like "Tarzan." It explained why they associated Africa with some negativity, but it did not account for all the hostility. Still, I could not resent them because I was aware of their long history of torment. They were also dealing with a myriad of social obstacles that gave them little room for contemplating details about post-colonial Africa. The issue was complex, and I could do little more than pray for their acceptance.

Even my fellow freshmen had other interests. There was a nice African American girl, who seemed to like me. Though we enjoyed each other's company, she would take off like a jet whenever her American friends came around. It was obvious to me that she felt embarrassed to be seen talking to an African. I was aware that my unruly hair and mismatched clothes made me look rather unattractive and out of place; my appearance was not a high priority, academics and my finances kept me busy.

Being on scholarship, I worried about whether I could maintain the required grade point to keep me in good standing. I had been secure in my academic abilities in Ghana, but I did not know what to expect at Bacchus. I had read that Americans were taught with the best teaching aids and facilities throughout high school. Would the background I had received at Oman be enough?

My confidence soared when the class material was familiar. I was surprised by how much information the professors provided - printed handouts, course packs, and teacher's notes. Used to completing courses without teachers, this information was heaven-sent. It made studying easier and more meaningful. The cost of textbooks, however, was horrendous. Five books cost me more than two hundred dollars – more than half my entire savings.

When I attended my first computer programming class, I had only seen computers through shop windows and in magazines; I had never used one. Now I had unlimited access to the real thing. The first assignment, in basic PASCAL, was ten pages. I did not understand a word of it, so I rushed to the computing center after class, but my apprehension got the better of me.

All the terrifying images I had conjured about ultra-smart American students and their ability to manipulate computers to do the unthinkable became real. The computer room looked like a hospital surgical ward. It was clean and brightly lit. Almost every computer station was busy with students engrossed in their projects. I saw engineering designs being modeled and rotated on different axes while other students typed quicker than I had ever seen.

The room buzzed with the soft chatter of the computer keyboards. No one noticed my puzzled stare. I stood alone feeling very disheartened. I had never even turned on a computer before. The facilitator pointed to a free computer terminal and walked away before I could ask any questions. I sat and stared at the unlit computer screen. Where was the switch? I thought. The instructions did not say. It seemed so basic that I was embarrassed to ask the students sitting closest to me. Such a revelation from a presidential scholar! After a couple of minutes, I slowly packed my book bag and left the computer room feeling inadequate - the first time I had backed away from an academic challenge. Did I have too much to learn to catch up? I could not afford anything less than an excellent grade if I wanted to keep my scholarship.

Fortunately, my Namibian friend Hafeni, who was experienced with computers - was in my class. Hafeni walked me through computing basics though he was tickled at my ineptitude. Once explained, the assignment was easy to manage. At the end of the term, my efforts were rewarded with an excellent grade. Overcoming the computer hurdle was a major victory; it set the stage for me to better handle subsequent challenges and gave me confidence in my ability to keep my scholarship. Having my academics under control was a good thing, but it brought my financial problems to the forefront.

All along, I suspected that the self-proclaimed philanthropist and loan shark Nii Ocansey, would not be dependable. My suspicions were confirmed when Mr. Ocansey failed to reply to numerous letters. As a fallback plan, I thought I could easily work to pay down my fees. If that did not work, I had assumed that I could join the track team and wrangle a sports scholarship. But how would I refund the airline ticket to my mother as promised? I had grossly miscalculated the depth of my financial problems.

Though the school was sympathetic, the best they could do was defer my payments and allow me to continue attending classes. I still needed to find a creative way to pay my tuition.

I applied to many private financial aid institutions to obtain funding. Though a vast amount of aid and scholarships were available for college students, it seemed they were all reserved for American citizens. Some grade requirements were quite low, but I knew I would not be eligible even if I earned a 4.0 grade point; I was not a permanent resident or a US citizen. When none of the fifty letters I sent responded favorably, I turned to work-study and sports programs.

At first, I was so thrilled with the idea of working that I took any job offered on campus. To make in one month what had taken me a whole year to earn during my national service was incentive enough. I washed dishes at the food service in the morning, guarded the Gymnasium in the evening, and then worked the midnight shift at the dormitory front desk - six days a week including weekends. I had assumed that work-study would be as manageable as my chores at Oman, but I was wrong.

During my first work week, I was too excited to feel fatigued. But as days turned into weeks, it dawned on me that I may have taken on more than I could handle. I worked at the food service from seven to nine in the morning, feeding dirty dishes onto a conveyor that ran through a gigantic stainless-steel dishwasher. By the second week, I hated that tormenting silver demon.

Once, I got a rush of dirty dishes and could not keep up with the clean ones exiting the dishwasher. Stacked plates and glasses accumulated until they started falling on the concrete floor. The clamor of broken glass and plates brought an angry supervisor who threatened to fire me if I could not keep up. To add to my frustration, my tireless Caucasian co-worker kept reminding me each time I tried to rest; "Gotta keep busy. Out here, ya just gotta keep busy," he said.

By the third week, I was fatigued from work, and the Physics class that followed was torturous. Now I thought the $3.35/hour wage was not enough; I was being driven into the ground at every job. I worked the dormitory front desk from one to six in the morning, leaving me barely an hour to shower and walk twenty minutes to down campus for my seven o'clock food service shift.

Gym guard duty was from six to nine at night. I watched over the equipment making sure no one was injured while exercising. Although it was the easiest job, I could not read because the supervisor had a way of showing up each night unannounced – and I did not want to risk losing my job.

After Gym duty, I spent the next three hours in the library

before returning to the dorm at midnight. That left me an hour to take a cat nap and get ready for my next job at the front desk at one. The exhaustive cycle repeated itself until I could catch up on my sleep when I was off duty from the front desk.

At minimum wage, I was turning in every cent over to the financial office, but I was not making a dent in what I owed the school. It seemed that after all the sleepless nights and hassle, I should have more than one hundred and fifty dollars every week. I could not make enough to cover my fees at that rate. Desperation began to set in. My options were running out. Nonstop letters from the financial office - demanding payment of my tuition and boarding balances - exacerbated my desperation. I was always expecting someone to say that I could no longer attend class. Getting another job was impossible. There were only twenty-four hours in a day, and as it was, I could barely afford a few hours of sleep a night.

I feared that the lack of sleep would catch up with me soon. I had to explore a sports scholarship. I had imagined that it would not take much to qualify for a track scholarship, but again, I was woefully misinformed. The stories I had heard at Oman about alumni financing their education with sports scholarships had omitted several important details.

Most accounts had implied that it was "easy" for Africans to excel in sports. All that it required was to be decent in a given sport. I figured that because I had run the cross-country for my dorm at Oman, I was qualified for college sports. I had gained a few pounds since coming to America, and distance running was no longer an option, so I opted for sprints. How difficult could it be? I wondered.

I discovered that college track was no trivial business. Practice was mandatory from three to five, Monday through Friday. For outdoor sprints, an athlete had to run a time of at least 10.50 seconds in the 100 meters to qualify for the NCAA conference meet and guarantee a track scholarship. This target could solve my financial woes, but I had never timed my sprints. I had no idea that it would require more than just raw ambition to achieve, so I temporarily wallowed in blissful ignorance.

On the first day of the fall indoor track practice, athletes were introduced and assigned their sports gear and lockers. I marveled at the camaraderie between the coach and athletes. We split into groups and the coach turned his full attention to the sprinters, his favorite. My teammates were unusually excited to have me on the team, but I began to panic when I found out why. Bacchus' last great track star was a Ghanaian who held the school record in the 100m! The coach and team believed that, being from the same country, I was their next track champion.

I reviewed the training itinerary in bafflement. First on the list was 2 miles easy at 50. I did not understand what the number 50 meant but shrugged it off feeling I could run with the best. It meant runners had to train at half their maximum effort for most of the run. When the eager coach decided to pace me with the team's best sprinters, reality set in, and the initial joy of being welcomed to the team vanished. The whistle blew and the sprint team was off to run 32 laps of the indoor track. The first couple was easy. I settled myself in front of the pack wondering why the others were so slow. I could hear the coach's voice urging us on, correcting our posture as we ran.

By the tenth round, I felt the first tinges of fatigue, but the rest of the team was just getting started. The pace continued to increase until I lost my rhythm. It was now an effort to keep up. What have I gotten myself into? I thought. With twenty laps still to go, I was trailing the pack. By the twenty-eighth lap, things were no longer funny. I was panting while the leading group had already lapped me twice, completing the run. The pain in my chest was unbearable and I searched for a clear spot to lay down my tortured body.

I tried to get off the oval track and onto the center field. When the coach and team members realized I was about to quit, they got in my way and started urging me on. "Way to go Kwei-si, you can do it, Kwei-si, you can do it!" they chanted. I wished they would shut up. I would have ignored them except they had formed a human wall along the inner lane preventing me from running off the track. I completed the last lap, alone, on the verge of collapse. After the run, I told the coach that I was out of shape and needed more training, but everyone knew that I was not going to be their next African champion.

The events at the first track practice were a precursor to two seasons of misery. Why I stuck with it was beyond me. Daily practice was no easy task. I suffered from painful shin splints and was prepared to take an extra shift at the food service instead of the rigorous training sessions, but I had to do both. No matter how hard I tried, I could not excel. The coach saw some promise in the 200 meters because I was always in the lead through the curve, but something always happened in the transition to the straightway; my feet literally buckled under me.

It was embarrassing when the team reviewed performance tapes. I would watch myself start well off the blocks, take the lead, and accelerate impressively through the curve. Then all of a sudden, I would slow down and appear to moonwalk backwards as the other runners slowly caught up and blazed past me. Sometimes I went from first to dead last at the finish line.

My best time in the 100m was pitiful and more than a second shy of the minimum required for the conference meet. I became filler material for the team at the weekend track meets. No one paid much attention to what I did. It was obvious that track was not the answer to my tuition problem. I simply lacked the talent to qualify for a scholarship. I worried that time was passing, and winter was fast approaching.

I had been looking forward to my first winter, but I soon discovered that, my body could not endure the cold winters of the American mid-west. While all the other students - including the Africans - dressed in heavy winter coats, I had to wear layers of sweaters to keep warm. Winter clothes cost a fortune and I could not afford them. When the temperatures dipped below freezing, layering sweaters did not work. Fortunately, my gracious host family came to the rescue.

The McKenzie family included Patrick, his wife, and Kelly their middle aged son. Patrick worked for the college and invited me to dinner whenever possible. They were warm, hospitable people. Their kindness was heaven sent. When they noticed my lack of appropriate winter wear, they showed up on campus one afternoon with my first winter coat. It was an old foam filled vinyl coat that had belonged to their son. Although it had busy yellow, pink, and purple stripes, I was very grateful for its warmth. The bitter cold had wiped out any vanity I possessed.

My first snow was beautiful. I had been studying in the library when I heard students playing outside. I was surprised at the bright white sheet that covered everything. It looked so pure and smooth that I reached down to touch the soft flakes. At the dorm, my roommate Chuck had organized a welcoming snowball party to celebrate my first experience.

I was jolted when the first snowball hit me square in the face, then Chuck and his friends hurled more balls at me. I was so thoroughly outnumbered that I could barely retaliate. I took things in good fun, but I was quietly steaming from my stinging face, freezing hands, and almost wet clothes. Some mischievous students in my dorm also had an annoying penchant for setting off the fire alarm when it was miserable outside. We had to evacuate the dorm until each room was inspected and cleared by the firemen. I could not think of an adjective low enough to describe the culprits while I stood in the cold with my teeth chattering.

Thinking only about the money, I accepted another job as a stand-by snow shoveler. It was only supposed to be on mornings when the sidewalks needed to be cleared before class. But the weather was cold and blustery when I was called. Wind chill temperatures were fifteen degrees below zero – forty-seven degrees below freezing. Within minutes, my fingers stiffened from the cold and refused to move.

My cheap gloves were too thin and unsuitable for outdoor work. When I blew warm air into my palms, my humid breath froze around my fingers causing more pain. I began to sense a stinging feeling in my almost numb ears. My nose began to run, and my physical motions were so painful that I quit before I got frostbite. I was not cut out for the cold harsh weather and took my name off the roster. It was the first job that I voluntarily quit even though it paid more than minimum wage.

I was glad when spring turned the corner and put an end to the miserable winter, but there was always something else to torment me. My second trimester at Bacchus was over, and I was feeling a little sorry for myself. Financial woes taunted me daily. My academic performance was the only thing that gave me comfort. My 4.0 GPA secured my scholarship for the year and prevented the school from kicking me out.

Sometimes I felt so alone. Chuck did not understand why I received no help from home. Most Africans on campus were supported either by their parents, or with scholarships from their countries. "Why don't you ask your parents for help?" He would say. But how could I ask for something they did not have? Even if they sold the house, they would not raise enough to pay my fees for four years. How was I to explain this to my colleagues? They had their own problems, and what Ghana's dilapidated economy had done to my parents' pension did not exactly make interesting conversation.

I had exhausted all my contingency plans. Sister Sena was helping as much as she could, but she was also pursuing her post graduate studies. She had taken loans to get this far and she was also trying to help the family in Ghana. There was really no more she could do. Each time a financial hold restricted my course registration, the school gave me a waiver. As the payments were deferred, my balance ballooned. I was at the end of my wits when I sought the advice of my guidance counselor. He suggested transferring to another college.

I pursued this vigorously. With my excellent academic record, I hoped to be more attractive to other institutions with better scholarship packages. I had completed applications to a few carefully selected schools, but financial aid decisions for transfer students would not be announced until mid-summer. All I could do was wait and leave the rest to providence.

During the third trimester, I opted out of the track team, but each day brought a host of new challenges. Letters from home had gradually stopped because I did not have time to write back. I thought about trying for jobs off campus, but found I could not possibly get to work without a car. There was also the problem of obtaining the legal permit from immigration to work off campus.

Kelly, my host brother, came to the rescue. Over the months, we had become close. Though Kelly's bushy mustache and ponytail made him easy to misjudge, he was the most caring and generous American I had met. He visited me often on campus riding his noisy Harley Davidson. Later that spring, he taught me how to drive a car and helped me get my driver's license. With his help, I also learned to ride a motor bike and experienced boating on the Mississippi.

When summer finally arrived, I needed to find a job off campus. Kelly found me a vehicle that fit my three hundred dollars budget - a rusty old 1973 Jeep with a dated orange hard top. Its steering had to be compensated for sudden swerves to the left when the brakes were applied. The ignition key no longer worked so I had to park on an incline each time I stopped so that I could push start the truck by myself.

Purchasing a car was one thing, but owning one was a different story. With little driving experience, my insurance was expensive. What I paid for a six-month policy was more than what I had paid for the Jeep. The registration and inspection tags blew more holes in my already tattered finances.

By the time I could legally drive the vehicle, the excitement over owning my first car had dissipated. Once, I thought owning a car would be the answer to my problems, but now I wondered. Would I ever be able to save any money at minimum wage? At least being mobile meant getting a better paying job off campus. Finding that "good job" was not easy. I had obtained a three-month work permit from immigration, but it still took weeks to get a job interview.

In the mean-time, I worked at the campus physical plant, reconditioning off campus apartments for the next fall term. My supervisor, who liked to be called "Crazy Rick," was a portly ex-marine and a taskmaster. Exotic animal tattoos covered both arms and his dark mustache made him look grumpy, mean and always angry. Everyone had to be promptly at work ten minutes before the official start time.

Each morning, he broke us into work teams sending fit workers on more physical assignments. I was always in that group. Working in warm weather did not bother me and the heavy work details meant I had a job through summer. Crazy Rick only fired those who could not work as hard.

I liked apartment cleaning the least because it sometimes

bothered my conscience. In some apartments, the residents had not taken their belongings with them. Whether they did this on purpose or not, I had no idea. I threw away closets full of clothes, pressing irons, stereos, couches, beds and all kinds of furniture.

I always asked Crazy Rick what to do with them and his answer was always the same, "Dump 'em, just dump 'em all." It bothered me because in Ghana, people worked several years to acquire these items. I knew many deserving people who could put them to good use. On one particular occasion, I was so dismayed that I found an excuse to be placed on another work detail.

Rick had sent us to install beds at the infirmary. The new electronically adjustable beds were to replace about twenty-five manually operated ones. The old beds were in pristine shape. Without doubt, they could be used elsewhere. When the new beds were in place, I asked Crazy Rick what to do with the old ones. "Dump 'em, just dump 'em all," was his response.

Crazy Rick could tell by the perplexed expression on my face that I was utterly confused. His next words made an attempt to explain. "There is no place to store them and it takes lots of time, paperwork, and lawyers to donate." I could think of many places in Ghana where the beds would have been welcome.

I was so sad after loading the beds in the truck that I asked Rick to assign me to another work group to avoid the actual dumping. I was ashamed of my helplessness. How could I dream of giving something back to my country if I was throwing everything in the garbage? What was my purpose in America when I could not even find a way to send the hospital beds to help my country? I tried to salve my guilt by collecting appliances and clothes, thinking I might have a few dollars one day to send them to Ghana. That day never came. I never thought I would be so wasteful.

Later that summer, I found a second job as a waiter at Rosetti's, a family-owned French-Italian restaurant near campus. I thought the manager hired me, because he had attended Bacchus too. It paid minimum wage, but I was encouraged by the prospect of making extra money in tips. When I accepted the position, I did not know I would be the restaurant's only black waiter and that some patrons would not like that.

I had never eaten in a restaurant like Rosetti's and did not know what comprised a four or six course meal. My experience with American food had been limited to the college cafeteria and fast food restaurants. In Ghana, I had seen McDonalds, Burger King, and Kentucky fried chicken commercials, and the food had made my mouth water.

I dreamed about tasting a McDonald's burger, or Kentucky fried chicken. But my first hamburger was tiny and too costly. It tasted just like the burgers at the campus cafeteria. Even the Big Mac could not appease my taste-buds. Kentucky Fried Chicken was the same – the chicken was not nearly as tasty as the home-bred fowls in Ghana. Several disappointing meals later, I gave up experimenting with food. I longed for some basic Ghanaian staples, like fufu, banku, gari and beans, which I had previously taken for granted.

I had been in the country for almost a year but knew relatively little about restaurant food. Waiting tables in an exclusive restaurant would not be easy. I took Rosseti's menu home after the first day and memorized it. Though unable to describe how a dish was prepared, I could repeat what was on the menu, and it worked because most people did not read their menus in detail. Over time, I learned how to balance large trays of food and needed little assistance to do my work, except for taking bar orders - the most challenging part of the job.

Almost all the drinks were new to me. I tried to cover up my lack of knowledge by phonetically writing what I thought I heard - fuzzy navel, screwdriver, bloody Mary, rusty nail, margaritas, and daiquiris. Usually, if I got half the name, the bartender could decipher what made little sense to me. I thought the world of her but there was a time when even she could not help me. My strategy failed when I thought "Carafe of Chablis" was the name of a drink when in fact, it was a measure of white Chablis wine.

The patron spoke fast. I was only able to get the word "Carafe" on the bar ticket but could not make out the other syllables. It took three trips between the bar and the serving table to get it right. Each time I returned to ask what kind of wine the customer wanted; she spoke too fast for me to understand. Finally, the irritated patron broke the order down into syllables; "I said, Ka-r-aff of Cha-b-lee. Got it, Cha-b-lee?"

Apart from learning about different foods, drinks and ice cream flavors, I ran into my first experience of overt racial prejudice. One evening, an elderly white couple sat at one of my tables. I handed them their menus and proceeded to welcome them to the restaurant. The couple was taken aback when they saw me and appeared uncomfortable. When they did not respond to my greeting, or to the question, "May I get you some drinks while you look at the menu?" I decided to give them some time. When I approached the table again, the man was waving frantically at the restaurant owner. By then, I understood what was happening and was not shocked when the manager insisted on being called if the couple ever sat at one of my tables again. My boss never explained the incident, but we both knew what had happened.

Similar situations followed, but I tried to keep focused on my goal. I just needed additional income to help pay my fees - I felt no desire to fight a battle I could not win.

Much as the owners liked me, it was not difficult to guess their choice between keeping me on the payroll and releasing me to please a loyal patron. I would not allow myself to get carried away by emotion, then lose my job and fail to save enough to return to school in the fall.

Some of my money paid my rent, fuel, insurance, and food, but most went back to the school. I was trying to clear my tuition balance before the fall semester, or a financial hold would prevent me from registering again. If I had to leave the school, I would lose my visa – and my campus employment - not to mention, what it would do to my education.

So, I took on a third job mowing a local cemetery lawn on weekends. The position offered almost twice the minimum wage, paid in cash and I could not refuse. I would never have had the courage to do this in Ghana, where the mores involving treatment of the dead were so delicate. Working in a cemetery required bravery and spiritual purity to avoid the apparent wrath of the ancestral gods. To protect myself from psychological repercussions, I avoided looking at the names on the headstones as much as possible.

I dared not write home about the depths to which I had sunk for fear of disappointing my family and friends who had placed so much faith in me. As an aspiring university student in Ghana, working in a cemetery was not what my parents envisioned. Survival now had made it an appealing solution. I prayed that I would soon see a ray of light coming through my dark tunnel of existence.

My prayers were finally answered when I received a transfer admission to a predominantly black college in Texas, which included a full-tuition award. I was as excited as the day I received my American visa. Now I appreciated the hardships that foreign students faced when college finances were not in order. I had survived the grueling year because of ambition and fear of failure. How long could I have kept going at such a pace? The new scholarship brought hope to a spirit dampened by strife.

For the first time since my arrival in America, I had something to celebrate. Without the burden of financial problems, I was able to enjoy the rest of the summer with my host family and Namibian friends. I had been on the verge of destruction but had discovered a deep inner strength and fortitude within myself that I never knew existed. Until some of the stress was lifted, I did not realize just how mentally exhausting living without leisure had been. God had been good to me and the reprieve was very welcome. I could now look forward to school in Texas.

When it was time to leave Illinois, I had saved a little money after selling the Jeep back to my host brother, Kelly. The vehicle could not make the 1500-mile journey to Texas. I was thankful to all those who had helped me start a new chapter in my life.

CHAPTER FIVE
Campus Life in Texas

I took in the large flat lands during the drive from the airport to the school campus and understood why "big" was synonymous with Texas. The expressway was lined with fenced ranches that stretched for miles. It was a scorching afternoon, but I welcomed the similarities to Ghana's tropical climate. Even with my limited exposure to American mid-western weather, I was willing to take a hot balmy day over a cold winter day, any time.

The campus had a welcoming aura that made me feel I had made the right decision. It was much larger than Bacchus, also well maintained, and dotted with several imposing brick buildings. During the short ride through the campus, I saw many well-polished, low-rider cars cruising the streets with stereos that had enough power to operate mini discos. Their deep thumping base rattled the taxi's loose panels as they drove by.

I noticed that most of the students were well-dressed, clean-cut African Americans. Judging from my own unsuccessful styling experiments, I wondered enviously how the young men shaped their hair with such precision - not a single strand was out of place. The college girls strutting along the sidewalks were breathtaking. I had not seen so many fine young black women in one place since my days at the university in Ghana. Thus far, everything about the school made me feel at home.

Within a week, I was able to delineate my existence into four experiences: administration, dormitory, academic, and social. The administration experience was similar to the way things were done in Ghana. We managed to get things done if we did not mind being given the run-around a couple of times or being admonished when we did not have the right paperwork. Dorm life, however, took a significant cultural adjustment.

All the students in my dorm were black, so I hoped the reception would be better than I received at Bacchus. I was assigned a room with two freshmen - one was Delmar, a curly haired talkative, from San Antonio. The other was Leroy, a handsome fellow from Houston who kept his head almost bald with just a hint of hair.

Delmar was easy going and the only one with any interest in Africa. Pretty boy Leroy never showed more than a cursory interest. He kept confusing Ghana with Guyana and often asked questions like; "Do you all have houses in Africa?" Or, "My mama said you all don't use deodorant in Africa, is that true?" If I was in a good mood, I would answer as best as I could, but sometimes, I ignored him so I would not blurt out something I would regret later. He was my roommate and we had to live together.

Every weekend, Leroy's dotting mother brought him

spending money and a week's supply of food and clean clothes. When she was around, Leroy behaved respectably, but when it came to college girls, he was something else. He had no difficulty approaching the opposite sex. It was a different girl everyday - so many of them that I lost count. I learned not to enter the room without jingling my keys or making some sort of noise. Sometimes, I would still walk into an embarrassing situation; then Leroy would be mad at me for days and place signs on his TV barring me from turning it on.

Somehow, we still managed to get along until Leroy's mother inexplicably bought him a handgun. I had met the single mother several times when she visited and knew that she loved her son dearly. However, when she tried to explain her actions, I was confused. "A guy needs some protection these days," she said. Did she mean protection from unarmed students? I did not understand. The gun did not improve Leroy's temperament. He became obsessed with staring, cleaning, and handling the silver .38 caliber pistol.

Before long, pretty boy's social life began to plummet. He went from occasionally smoking marijuana to a chronic addiction. He spent more time in the room with a towel placed under the door to prevent the distinctive aroma of weed from filtering into the hallway. I began to worry because Leroy was getting more irritable and had started to hang out with another dorm clown on crack cocaine.

Leroy slept with his gun under his pillow and got jumpy when anyone entered the room. The girls, I could deal with, but his paranoia was too much for me; no telling what Leroy would do next. What if there was a security raid? I doubted if anyone would understand that I was simply there for an education, not to use drugs. I had to do something, so I tried to get reassigned to a different room.

The meeting with the resident director was disappointing.

I told him that I was not getting along with my roommate but did not mention the gun - in case I was tempting fate. I was informed that room changes during the semester were impossible without an attempt to arbitrate. I did not want Leroy to know that I was scared. I knew my faked "Mandingo" African warrior demeanor was the only thing keeping the paranoid pretty boy at arm's length. What if he denied having a gun? I had no desire to provoke Leroy into doing anything that could harm me, so I decided to wait out the last month of school.

By the end of the semester, I was convinced that Leroy was hooked on something. Missing were the pretty girls, the clean clothes, and daily haircuts. In their place were desperate looking girls, messy clothes and hair, and a pretty boy in free fall. I spent my time away from the dorms - at work, studying, or visiting other classmates.

The next semester, my roommates were Djuan a religious sophomore from Dallas, and a big guy who called himself Mad Dog. Looking at Mad Dog alone was scary. The football player stood well over 6 feet with muscles bulging through all his clothes.

Mad Dog was rarely alone. He was always surrounded by friends. I called them "Mad Dog's fan club." He did not seem to care about dorm rules. He filled all the available shelve space in the room with empty liquor bottles - a fact that neither Djuan nor I had the nerve to question. Mad Dog did not drink or use drugs but he seemed to have no problem letting his friends do whatever they pleased. They ignored me most of the time and later, I learned that they thought I was just another guy who had come to America to take opportunities away from African Americans. I was still struggling for my existence and did not know how to respond.

One Saturday night I had been studying late and arrived

at the dorm after two in the morning. Mad Dog was gone. Djuan was still poring over his bible. We exchanged small talk, then prepared to turn in. Half an hour later, loud banging on the door woke me. A jerry-curled man dressed in all black with heavy gold chains around his neck and wrists was leaning on the wall across the narrow hall. He stared down at me with half closed blood shot eyes, reeking of tobacco and alcohol. I doubted if he was a resident. "Where Mad Dog?" He asked in a hoarse yet commanding voice. Adrenaline shot through my veins. Was the man there to cause trouble or for a friendly visit? "He is not here right now." I said.

Mr. Jerry Curls leaned over and lowered his voice almost to a whisper. "Do you have a dime for me?" He asked. I did not understand what he meant, but I wanted to get him away from the door. Thinking he was asking for money, I fetched my wallet and offered him a dollar. The gesture seemed to really upset Mr. Jerry Curls. "Are you trying to be funny or what?" He said.

Djuan took the man aside in the hallway and quieted him after a few moments. Then he turned and walked down the hall swaying from side to side like a pendulum. Djuan noticed my confused expression and said, "I think Mad Dog has been selling crack cocaine. A dime is ten dollars of the drug." "If anybody knocks like that again, ask them who they want and don't open the door if Mad Dog isn't here." Djuan could see through Mad Dog's act because he had grown up in a tough Dallas neighborhood, but I remained very uneasy.

My next roommate proved that Leroy and Mad Dog were aberrations. Damon was an Army ROTC cadet officer, very disciplined and religious. He was so neat and organized that I had to work hard to keep up. I learned a lot from the soft-spoken African American, and things were wonderful until the Gulf War broke out. It was sad to say good-bye to my best roommate after he was called into active duty in Saudi

Arabia.

We were the same age, and the situation made me think about the challenges that Damon would face at war, not to mention the risk to his life. I felt respect for the quiet African American soldier who had briefly touched my life and was frustrated that I could do little more than wish him well. After that experience, I decided to rent an apartment off campus. The emotional roller coaster involved with different roommates was too harrowing; I needed to concentrate on my schoolwork.

Academic life in Texas was unique in its inclusion of Afrocentric studies. Although some people thought the curriculum lacked the aggressive competitiveness of larger universities, I believed it provided an excellent education for anyone willing to work hard. For minorities it was an academic haven away from the more distracting social issues of racism and prejudice.

The lectures on race, ethnicity, and African American history gave me rare insight into issues I previously knew very little about. I learned about the courageous lives of Booker T. Washington, W.E.B. Dubois, Martin Luther King Jr., Malcom X, and Rosa Parks. I realized that my current opportunity was linked to the Civil Rights advances they fought and died to create. I knew how different conditions could be in another institution and was grateful to the great people who had made it possible for me to attend university. Their struggles also helped me better understand black people in America. It made me more tolerant of Leroy's indifference and the hostility from Mad Dog and his friends.

Even so, I was ambivalent about my academic success. I was performing above average in my class and knew that I would be looked on favorably when it came time to hire. I had worked hard to excel, but how could I find joy if I could be taking an opportunity away from another? Was

I doing something wrong by sacrificing so much for my academic ambitions? These conflicting emotions plagued me throughout my university stay. I found a little consolation in knowing that academic performance correlated with government grants, and I was helping to sustain the opportunity for other generations of minorities.

Most of the faculty was intelligent African Americans who had been trained in the country's best institutions. A few foreign faculty – including Ghanaians, Nigerians, and Jamaicans – had brought the rigorous structure of the British system to the engineering and science programs. Their courses were not easy to pass, and students did everything to avoid them.

There was a Ghanaian professor, who was so strict that he had no qualms failing any student, including graduating seniors. Unhappy students went to great lengths to express their frustration. I often wondered why he had to park his car on the campus police lot.

The large number of female students in engineering and math impressed me. They were very competitive students who made me earn every grade I made. There were also several African American men who were dedicated to their education. The loud music and low rider cars were deceptive. Most students were working in earnest toward a better future.

The campus was always alive with fun and activities. Many active fraternities and sororities held functions every day of the week. I was too busy to participate, but sometimes I watched the frat brothers enviously while they performed stepping acts with canes they twirled around in synchronized motions. I wanted so much to be a part of a fraternity, but I did not know how and lacked the time for the demanding pledging process.

Caribbean students were the second largest group on campus. They were highly driven students. They dominated the school's track team with their unique athletic abilities. Their parties, however, were not for the timid. They were wild and enjoyable. Even the overzealous campus police did not dare interrupt their functions. They reminded me of my proud Namibian friends, Hafeni and Sheya.

Though Africans were a relatively smaller group, I had never seen so many from different countries in one place. Almost every country in the Sub-Saharan region was represented - Liberia, the Senegal, the Gambia, Sierra Leone, Ghana, Nigeria, the Cameroon, Ethiopia, Sudan, Somalia, Uganda, Kenya, Tanzania, Zimbabwe, and South Africa. We all shared collective activities through the campus African Students Association.

The Liberians were the largest group, but the Nigerians were the most dominant and charismatic Africans on campus. They worked as hard at their academics as they did at having fun. While most Africans drove beat-up cars, they drove Cadillacs, BMWs, Mercedes, and Jaguars. I had no idea where they got their money, but they came to class in fashionable designer clothes, greeting each other by calling out, "Niger Power!" They were also generous people. On many occasions, I was invited to join my Nigerian classmates in Houston to have some fun. When I needed a job in the city, I was grateful for their help; they were masters in the art of survival.

My closest friend, Kamau was from Kenya. The Kenyans' hearty sense of humor made them fun. But I avoided getting involved when they "caned" each other. That was when friends got together and made merciless fun at anyone who had been caught in a recent blunder. Though their jokes were hilarious, they were sometimes cruel and I was not sure I could stomach being the brunt of such jokes.

The strength of the African women impressed me the most. Despite some of the cultural limitations they faced, it was comforting to see that they refused to be outdone. They were industrious to a fault. Akosua Manu was a Ghanaian whose academic prowess equally frustrated and motivated us. She was a powerhouse who had successfully dealt with the same cultural upheavals that we had and seemed to be doing a lot better. She had an impressive academic record and showed leadership in several campus organizations. She also found the time, on occasion, to invite us over to enjoy a home-cooked African meal. Most of us were in awe of her, but never told her for fear that she might take advantage of our admiration.

Even with all the different nationalities, the social and academic environment was unthreatening. It allowed committed minority students to comfortably compete for access to honorary professional and academic societies. In my engineering program, it transformed job placement into an exciting experience. It was comforting to know that recruiting companies were hiring the best students on campus, so different from Bacchus where I was never called back after interviewing with several companies.

I knew that if I landed a job, I would need a reliable means of transportation - nothing like the Jeep I drove in Illinois. So, my first summer was spent saving for a car. I stayed with Sister Sena who graciously helped me save on rent. I worked three jobs. I ran the cash register at an art supply store until five in the evening, and then rode my bike to the gas station where I worked from six to midnight. During the weekends, I worked at the store and cooked pizzas at a Pizzeria until midnight.

Each day at the gas station was a challenge. My Korean boss openly disliked African Americans. He told me that he had only hired me to satisfy a management order to diversify his work force. It did not make my life any easier. I also found out that I had replaced another worker who had been stabbed to death in a recent robbery attempt. I almost quit, except I was not sure I could find another job that was as convenient in a short time. I could only pray to God for protection.

The most annoying part about working at the gas station was dealing with con artists. When a gentleman in a Porsche claimed he had left his wallet at his apartment, I did not think that anyone driving such an expensive car would be hard pressed to cough up fifteen dollars for gas. I allowed the man to leave after taking his name and phone number. He never returned and the phone number was fabricated. The money, however, came out of my pocket.

Another couple came by when the station was busy on the pretext of needing change. While I counted out the money, they changed their minds twice, requesting change for a different amount - each time confusing me in the process. I felt something was wrong, but the station was too busy for me to dwell on it for long. It was not until they were long gone that I realized I had given them more money than I received. The unfortunate trend continued through the summer and I found myself becoming very suspicious of my customers.

Despite these minor setbacks, I achieved my goal and bought a decent looking Nissan Sentra to help me commute between school and work. This time, the car had moderate miles and none of the problems that my first jeep had. I rented an off-campus house with a couple of African students and looked forward to the next semester as a welcome break from working100-hour weeks all summer long. But my newly found mobility made me the target when any of my housemates needed transportation. It took a close entanglement with the law, to remind me of how easy it was to get into real trouble; especially in a State where the motto is, "Don't mess with Texas"

Early one Saturday morning, Usmanu, one of my African

roommates called to be picked up from work. Usmanu's car had broken down so I agreed to help. When we got close to campus, it was after six in the morning. I was still slightly groggy. At Usmanu's insistence, I stopped for some gas. I stood casually aside while Usmanu pumped the gas and paid little attention until I noticed the cash indicator roll past the amount Usmanu had paid the cashier.

When I asked him to stop pumping, Usmanu argued that it was the gas station's responsibility to set the pump's auto shut-off. My angry expression made him let up on the pump handle. The indicator stopped at $5.63 but Usmanu had no more money on him. I would have paid the 63 cents myself, but I did not have it either. I made a mental note to return to the station later with the money as we drove back to campus. I was too upset at Usmanu to say a word.

I was probably not as alert as I thought because it did not cross my mind, to consult with the cashier before leaving. Big mistake! Instead, I took the back roads to campus and unleashed my frustration by driving like a maniac ignoring all the speeding regulations along the way. When I got to campus, a squad car with lights flashing was waiting at the main intersection.

Usmanu and I were made to straddle the hood while we were searched. The scene was degrading and embarrassing as other students slowed down to gawk at us. It had not dawned on me what was happening. I thought the police had clocked me at a high rate of speed and would charge me with reckless driving. Then the police officer said, "What did you boys do at Petrol-Mart?"

"We went to get some gas." I said. We were escorted back to the gas station in trouble for the 63-cent over-pump. The owner decided to press full charges. Since students had run off after pumping several gallons of gasoline before, she refused any type of payment we offered. We continued to the police station, and I realized we were in deep trouble. The lady, who owned the gas station, wanted to make an example of us and was going to make sure we went to jail!

They had to wake up the judge for the arraignment. By the time they started questioning me, I was beside myself with anxiety. Oh no, I thought, I am going to jail! What kind of thanks does one get from helping people these days? What would this do to my parents? I could hear the rumor mill now; "Did you hear that Kwesi was sent to America to go to school, but instead of studying, he got caught for stealing 63 cents." What a disgrace! Who could I call to bail me out? I hoped the bail money was not so high that I would have to seek help from home.

Just when they were about to take my thumbprints, Usmanu admitted to the Judge that he was the one who had pumped the gas. They released me and arrested him. After listening to our story, the judge called the station owner again, but she still refused to drop the charges. The sympathetic judge gave Usmanu two years probation; his record would be expunged if he stayed out of trouble. He also told us that he was only giving us consideration because we came across as being honest and remorseful. We walked out of the police station feeling as though we had just gone ten rounds with a heavy weight champion - a harrowing experience for both of us.

I had mixed feelings about the incident. Sixty-three cents did not seem like a lot, but I respected the American justice system and how quickly the police responded when called upon. We could have been in more serious trouble and appreciated the judge's leniency. I swore to pay attention to the basic tenets of right and wrong that my parents had taught me. For me, the experience brought new meaning to the term, "Don't mess with Texas."

My junior year was in full swing. With a reliable car, I

began exploring prospects for, an engineering internship and signed up for interviews with a few companies. I had little experience with the formal interview process and found that academic excellence alone was not enough to secure the jobs I wanted. I needed relevant experience and involvement in activities that showed I was well rounded.

I had the grades and the experience from my numerous jobs, but lacked involvement in extracurricular activities, so I joined a couple of societies on campus. I got to know more people, while organizing fundraisers and academic competitions. It added spice to my professional development, but the dues hit my pockets hard. How was it that everything in America boiled down to money? Although I understood that the benefits of membership provided more than the token fees, I was going broke rapidly.

The next hurdle was my attire. I had not paid much heed to my appearance in years. After watching other students dressed in sharp suits for their interviews, I knew that I also needed new clothes and a decent haircut. The only way I could afford a new suit was from the Ice Man. Ice was the "sell-everything" connection man on my floor when I lived in the dorms. Nobody asked where he got the stuff, but he would take orders during the week and have it by the weekend, price tags and all.

Fifty dollars solved the suit problem. Six dollars and an appointment with Styles, the most popular barber on campus took care of my nappy hair. The hole in my pocket was burning deeper. I had never spent so much on myself, let alone on a job prospect with no guarantees. I realized, however, that it was a necessary transition in my professional growth. Gone was my crude country appearance. Now I looked sharp, well groomed, and ready for a professional assignment.

I had great respect for those who had landed good jobs. It

was no easy task. Good grades and experience I understood but selling myself to strangers was totally new to me. There was another handicap to overcome - I needed to apply for an extension of my temporary work permit from the immigration office - another headache I could do without.

To me, interviewing was a necessary evil. My first few experiences were terrible because I did not understand appropriate interview protocol. I was unaware that they evaluated posture, and communication skills in detail. Getting used to wearing the suit and tie was another issue altogether. As with previous challenges, I watched others and asked the successful ones for help. My future depended on it. With practice, the questions became more familiar and I got better. Several rejection letters later, I received my first offer from Gittannes Automotive Components, a parts manufacturer, and I was off to Detroit for my first engineering summer assignment.

CHAPTER SIX
Summer in the Midwest

Finding suitable accommodations in a city where I did not know a soul was risky business. I did not consider that I might end up in an undesirable part of town, or with people who had unusual inclinations. I relied solely on recommendations from the corporation's student programs office to find a place to live. Being an industrial city, the cost of living in Detroit was relatively high. For my three-month internship, I could not afford the monthly rent of a decent apartment, and few desirable places would allow a short lease. That left me with renting from employees of the corporation. It seemed to be an excellent program.

Gittannes' directory of prospective homeowners with rooms to let included such information as distance to work, room size, rent, and house rules. I selected a house on Detroit's east side. If I had any idea what that part of the East Side was like, I might have reconsidered. "Three-bedroom colonial house, only one block from the Detroit River overlooking Windsor, Canada. Two rooms available, 25 minutes to work." Rent was comparatively affordable. After phoning the homeowners, Bernie and Dan, I was sure it would be fine. I even convinced my Kenyan friend Kamau – who had also landed a summer job in Detroit - to rent the other room so we could live together.

The interstate maps were easy to follow, and we arrived in Detroit after driving for almost 24 hours. As we made our way through the downtown district, I marveled at the tall renaissance center, the size of the Cobo hall, and the commemorative Joe Louis sports arena. It was a nice Saturday afternoon and most commercial businesses were closed. We headed further east on Jefferson and the scenery changed dramatically. Several buildings had been abandoned while broken windows and graffiti walls told a doleful story. From the number of loiterers and jalopies I realized we were "in the hood."

We finally arrived at a beautiful red brick house. Although it sat right in the middle of the hood, I did not mind because most people I saw were black. How different could they be from those I had met in Texas? I had made enough friends there to realize that most Texans were good people with big hearts and I had developed a sixth sense for recognizing those I needed to stay away from.

My landlords were characters themselves. Bernie, in his mid-fifties, worked for Gittannes and had placed the ad for the rooms. Bernie was always eager to engage anyone in conversation. Dan was a quiet electrician at a local utility company. He was much younger than Bernie but appeared more assertive.

We moved in not suspecting anything different about their lifestyles. Bernie and Dan liked to cook so there was always lots of food in the house. They insisted on having Kamau and I home for dinner after work. We did not mind adhering to this house rule because our hosts were excellent cooks. Being close to the river was true, but I discovered that it was no place for sane people. Years of neglect had turned it into a prime location for drug trafficking, and the police constantly patrolled the area.

Neither Kamau nor I paid much attention when Bernie refused to talk about his family, or when their favorite movie was "Chariots of Fire," a story about male Olympic athletes. Even the fact that they were the only Caucasian residents on the entire street, or our inability to carry on a conversation with any of our neighbors, did not ring any bells. Each time, we drove up, Kamau and I felt curious eyes following us — several weeks later, we began to think otherwise.

Kamau stopped showing up for dinner or eating anything Bernie and Dan offered him. This went on for about a week, and I could pry no information from my friend. Kamau was a free spirit who did not like to be controlled, so I figured that either Bernie or Dan had said or done something to upset him. I decided to leave the matter alone until Kamau was ready to talk, it did not take long.

Kamau slept upstairs sandwiched between the master bedroom, where Bernie and Dan slept, and the bathroom at the end of the hall. I listened as Kamau recounted what had transpired about two weeks earlier. It was a hot and humid summer night and Kamau was having trouble sleeping. Since the room had no air conditioning, he opened the windows and cracked open his door to increase circulation.

He was awakened later by strange sounds coming from the master bedroom. He could hear moans and the rhythmic squeak of their king-sized bed. Kamau - who had grown up in very modest African surroundings - did not know what to make of those noises. His initial shock turned into discomfort, as the unwelcome noises continued to rob him of any sleep. The thought of shutting the noise out by closing the door was tempting, but the door hinges creaked too loudly. The sounds finally subsided and he heard one of the men walking down the hall towards the bathroom. As he passed Kamau's door he belched loudly. Kamau's imagination got the better of him and he could not bring himself to eat their food anymore.

It was never the same in the house after that, even though I was more tolerant of the two men. Now I understood why our neighbors avoided us and why two unlikely characters wound up living in the hood surrounded by black people. It made sense why Bernie would not talk about his family. We became rather guarded about our interaction with our landlords, especially, when Bernie walked into the bathroom while either Kamau or I was showering.

The situation got worse when I invited a female friend over. Bernie and Dan were so upset that they asked her to leave - so much for good relations. If we could have found other accommodations, we would have moved - but we had to tough it out for a few more weeks until school started.

In the end, I concluded that the two men were good people and had not meant any harm. If only Kamau had not heard them, it might have turned out great. I had to accept that my ignorance was mostly to blame for my anxiety. In a strange way, I was thankful for the experience. I felt better equipped to understand others with alternative lifestyles in the future. Bernie and Dan had offered us their hospitality. Their gracious meals were certainly the best I had eaten since arriving in America. It was their accommodation that enabled Kamau and I to complete a valuable internship experience that summer.

My first experience working for corporate America held lots of surprises. I learned to "play ball." Corporate culture had written and unwritten codes about dress, etiquette, how to talk to the boss, and how to conduct business over the phone. Inexperienced interns like me were immersed into this culture to transform us into consummate professionals. How well we did depended on our interpersonal skills and academics.

On the first day, I spent several minutes going from one gray building to the next until I arrived at the building where I was to report for work. The huge technical facility and spaghetti roadways made it difficult to recognize the buildings from the directions I was given. I noticed several of the company's products displayed around the polished entrance hall. It was impressive. Gittanes manufactured anything from tiny machine screws to huge diesel engines for locomotives.

Everyone was in a hurry. As I walked through the brightly-lit hallways, some smiled and nodded a greeting, but I was left feeling that most were reflex actions rather than genuine salutations. Everything was formal. The men wore dark suits or crisp white shirts and bright ties. I had worn my best plaid shirt and a black tie. Even though my pants were black, I had failed the dress code. I should have worn the suit I bought from Ice.

When I entered the orientation room, I discovered that the few interns wearing the wrong work attire were also minorities. No one had told us how to dress and act on the first day of work. I did not know them, but I was sure their credentials were exceptional to have landed a job with Gittannes. There would be a steep learning curve for some of us.

Most of the Caucasian interns wore professionally laundered clothes and carried black and brown leather planners. They asked most of the questions, the depth of which showed they had prior knowledge of the organization.

I knew little about the company's corporate structure and hesitated to ask questions, not wanting to make a fool of myself. Having relatives in the corporate world would have meant, being better prepared for this cultural shock. I wondered why Bernie had not explained the corporate culture to me in more detail but decided to visit the mall on my way home. I would not blow my golden opportunity over something so easily remedied.

We went through almost two hundred pages of material very quickly. Then I was directed to report to my assigned department - a division that designed and manufactured shock absorbers and other suspension components. At the entrance, I met my new manager – a woman. I was both shocked and impressed. She exuded confidence and was extremely effective at multi-tasking. In addition to being a Rhodes Scholar, she had a technical degree from the Massachusetts Institute of Technology. She was never too busy to answer my questions and her guidance and encouragement bolstered my own confidence. I was fortunate to have her as my first boss.

The next few weeks on the job, I was briefed about the departmental goals and their famous "mission statement." I attended many technical meetings, some lasting up to eight hours. I heard presentation upon presentation and acronym after acronym. It seemed the corporation, had its own language. I was very confused. It often took all my willpower to stay awake through the marathon meetings. Compared to working at minimum wage jobs, the physical pressure was much less, but the mental pressure was cranked way up.

My assignment required the redesign of a die used to manufacture a suspension component. It was a challenge. I had taken several design classes, but I was not sure where to begin. Why had they assigned such a "big" project to a "small" guy like me? Were they expecting me to screw up? Or worse, setting me up for a fall? I could not afford failure, so

I started to pay closer attention at the meetings until things began to make some sense.

I received a lot of help from my manager and other engineers. Success in my department depended on teamwork. Eventually, I began to feel confident enough to offer my opinion without hesitation. The next time I was under pressure again, I had been asked to make a final presentation about my findings - uncharted territory for me.

I had never faced so many professionals before. Gitannes' engineers knew their jobs well and did not hesitate to throw darts at a presenter if they felt that his information was incomplete or inaccurate. I had witnessed such theatrics all summer. Fearing that I would make a fool of myself, I memorized all fifteen slides of presentation material.

No amount of memorization, however, could quiet my nerves on presentation day. In the small conference room, I recognized only half of the ten engineers present. My throat was parched, and my voice sounded hoarse and alien even to myself. My hand shook very badly each time I changed my slides. The overhead projector magnified my shaky motions and cast strange cascading shadows on the projection screen each time I reached across the lens.

I had hoped to give the performance of my life so I could secure an invitation to work the following summer. Things were not going as planned. A fellow intern had told me to act as though I knew what I was talking about, even if I did not feel that way. Somehow, the faked confidence helped me present technically sound recommendations on how to improve the die's efficiency.

When the presentation was over, one engineer offered me an additional tip for controlling my nerves. "Water," he said, "Drink lots of water before your presentation." I would have done anything to avoid repeating the day's proceedings. Fortunately, my compelling arguments got rave reviews and earned me a second internship the following year.

That day signified a milestone in my journey toward professional maturity and brought a successful end to an eventful summer. My first exposure to corporate America had been good. I would be returning to college a more mature person.

CHAPTER SEVEN
A Summer to Remember

Having the promise of a good job did not necessarily bring peace of mind. It left me open to other problems, especially those related to owning a car. What I learned about driving in America, strengthened my faith in God. I was convinced that foreigners had guardian angels that took care of them every time they braved the freeways.

It was finals week, the end of the fall semester after my internship. I had been studying all day on Saturday. By eleven that evening, I was tired. Instead of going to bed, I thought that a drive would restore my concentration. It never occurred to me that my weary mental state was not conducive to driving.

Fifteen minutes later, I was on the freeway, driving around the hilly Texas countryside. There were cattle ranches on each side of the highway. Adrenaline coursed through my veins as

I sped past 80mph. Relishing the foolish rush that came with breaking the speed limit, I continued to push my little car. The night was pitch black, so I kept my eyes trained on the dashed lane divider for guidance.

With few cars on the road, I maneuvered my car around tight corners. I blew past slower traffic and attacked the hills like a roller coaster. Sometimes the gradients were so steep that I could not see past the hilltops. My heart pounded each time I crested the hills wondering what to expect on the other side - it was risky and exciting at the same time.

I turned the car around but, the drive back was somehow different. The night seemed darker and the lane divider, nothing but a thin continuous line. My blurry vision should have cautioned me that I was getting tired and driving too fast. But I was beyond rational thinking. As I crested the last hill, I came upon a gigantic white obstruction straddling my lane. I was confused. Was the still figure a live horse or my imagination? The next thing I remembered was white oblivion.

I must have been out for only a few seconds because when I regained consciousness, the car was still moving - it had crossed the median and was now facing oncoming traffic. It was difficult to see because the windshield was in a million pieces flapping against the wheel. I frantically tried to maneuver the car away from the fast-approaching headlights. I felt the skin around my knuckles peel off as the sharp edges of the shattered windshield sliced into them. The wheel got slippery, but I was too frightened to feel any pain. All I could do was point the car away from the traffic and back into the median.

When the car finally stopped in the mushy median, I tried to get out, but none of the doors could open. Being trapped in the dark confines of the mangled car was frightening. What if the car burst into flames? I kicked the windshield until I could crawl out and began running around the vehicle in a daze. Fortunately, other cars stopped to offer their assistance. They advised me to stay still to avoid further injuries. Within seconds, sharp pains overcame me in my back. The reality of what had just happened began to sink in. The white image had been no illusion – I had run into a horse!

Minutes later, the dark night was consumed by the drama of flashing lights from the emergency vehicles – police, fire, ambulance, and salvage. There was a dead horse, a totaled car, and an injured driver. I was glad to see help come my way but remained in a daze as I struggled to answer questions for the police and medical personnel. Everything was happening so fast that it frightened me.

The ride to the hospital took an eternity. My head was pounding, and my back was painfully sore. What would happen to me? Was I seriously hurt? I had no medical insurance. How would my family react if they heard I had been injured in an accident? I felt a deep pain in my heart as I thought about my mother. Much as I wanted to share my pain, I did not want her to worry and made up my mind to keep this to myself.

At the hospital, I was x-rayed and told I had no serious injuries. A sigh of relief was all I could manage. My voice was hoarse from the shards of broken glass lodged in my throat. Bruised muscles around my spine caused the back pain, and the headache was a result of trauma to my head as the horse slid over the roof. When I was discharged, I was glad to see my friend Kamau in the waiting room. It had been quite a night.

I struggled through the finals week in physical and mental agony. I tried to ignore the pain so I could concentrate on my exams. When my friends found out that I had run into a horse, they thought it was hilarious. I was not amused. "How could you hit a horse?" they would ask. "What were you smoking that night?" "Didn't you see the horse?" "How long have you had your driver's license?" "Is the horse all right?" They seemed more interested in the horse than my pain. I wanted to scream in frustration. No one believed that a collision between an animal and an automobile could be serious. Even Kamau thought my pain was exaggerated until he saw the damaged car.

We had gone to the junkyard to retrieve my personal effects. The front end of my car was mangled steel. Except for a bulge where the horse slid over my head, the roof had caved in and all the windows were smashed. Kamau said my head must be as hard as steel. There was white horsehair caught in the mangled metal and I felt sorry for the horse.

The owner of the ranch filed a suit to recover damages for the horse because I was speeding, and because the ranch had been fenced according to state specifications. Not only was I being bombarded with medical bills from the ambulance and emergency service, I had to find money to pay for the horse. I was not amused. If anything, I blamed the ranch owner for allowing the horse to stray onto the highway.

I was working myself into a mental frenzy when I realized how close I had come to losing my own life. Assigning blame no longer seemed important. Fortunately, my auto insurance paid for everything including the damages claimed by the rancher. What would I have done without it? Someone was surely watching over me.

It took a few months, but I fully recovered, and by the end of the spring semester of 1991, I was in high spirits again after acing all my engineering courses. I had bought another car with the insurance settlement and my bank account was healthy. I also had a well-paying summer internship lined up at Gittannes for the second consecutive year.

This time, I had pre-arranged accommodations in Hazel Park, far from Bernie and Dan. I had prepaid the first month's rent and was looking forward to an enjoyable summer. But things started going wrong a week before I was due to leave for Detroit. I was driving back to the school campus on the one-mile entrance road. There were a couple of cars ahead of me, and the smoke from the popular campus barbecue drifted across the street. Through the haze, I noticed that the tiny red car ahead of me had stopped to make a left turn.

Who was crazy enough to stop in the right lane of a 35mph speed zone? The traffic behind me was moving briskly and it would not have been wise to stop. So I switched lanes to pass the vehicle but the little red car suddenly turned into my lane and stopped again. I hit my brakes and rubber squealed as I desperately tried to stop the vehicle. Bang! I was not hurt, but I knew I was in trouble. I got out of the car steaming and upset.

The driver was my friend Akosua Manu. A couple of weeks earlier, I had tried unsuccessfully to teach her how to drive. So, to see her behind the wheel of a car without an instructor was shocking - I could understand why she was driving that way. "Are you all right?" I asked. She smiled sheepishly and nodded. Her car was barely scratched, but mine was badly damaged; oil and other fluids were dripping to the ground.

The law was clear about rear end collisions; I was at fault. A second incident within the same year would taint my driving record even further and push my insurance premium even higher. I was in no mood to face the police. Moreover, I doubted if Akosua had a license and did not want to see my friend in trouble. Since no one was hurt and there was nothing wrong with her car, we did not wait for the police.

Without a police report, there could be no help from my insurance. It confounded me that this had happened the first time my bank balance was in the black. Now I hoped the repair would not be too expensive, or it would be the end of my summer job. Welcome to America, where fortunes change by the minute.

Kamau introduced me to Carlos, a fast-talking Mexican mechanic who was cunning and unpredictable. His estimates changed with his mood, but he was good, and sometimes, he gave students a break. Upon inspecting the car, Carlos said, "I thought you said it was just a small job; this will cost you at least seven hundred dollars." Almost the sum total of my bank balance. I pleaded, begged, moaned, and implored, but Carlos would not budge. I spent the week in Houston getting the car repaired - so much for visiting my host parents in Illinois as I had planned.

On my way to Detroit, I was stopped by the police and fined for speeding. The ticket wiped out all my cash because it had to be paid before I would receive my first paycheck. Usually, I enjoyed long driving trips, but I was miserable. I had no money and only a credit card with a $500 limit. I had to rely on credit for gasoline and food.

Living on credit was not very smart especially when I could not remember my PIN number to draw cash advances. Fast food restaurants did not accept credit and a five-dollar burger and fries at McDonalds was ten dollars at the Country Steak House. The food was good but there was little pleasure in eating beyond my means. At least my first month's rent had been paid.

I arrived in Detroit late Sunday prior to my scheduled start for the summer internship. I was unaware that Hazel Park was predominantly Caucasian. My roommates were five other Gittannes interns from different parts of the country. That they were all Caucasian should have raised a red flag in my mind, but I was too preoccupied with my immediate problems to see the Mack truck heading toward me at full speed.

The following day, I arrived at the house to find Mr. Landlord, his wife, and two other men waiting for me. My hearty hello was met with a stifled grunt from Mr. Landlord; the rest did not bother to respond. Though I was no stranger to offhand treatment from some Caucasians, I sensed that something was seriously amiss. Still, in the interest of harmony, I decided to ignore the incident. The air was thick with tension, and when the landlord summoned me into the kitchen, I followed apprehensively.

Nothing prepared me for what this man who worked for Gittannes had to say. "I don't want any trouble with the NAACP (National Association for the Advancement of Colored People), or from Gittannes. But I've got to tell you, the neighbors are complaining about your presence in this house." I had only been there less than twenty-four hours. Was it possible that I had already turned the neighborhood upside down?

Mr. Landlord claimed that members of the Ku Klux Klan lived in the neighborhood and, an African American couple had been recently run out of the neighborhood by death threats and damage to their property. "I would have told you when you called on the phone, but I thought you were Filipino or something." He said. "I'm not asking you to move, but if you decide to leave within the next day or so... I'll refund your rent check." When he stopped talking, an eerie silence filled the kitchen.

I got the message – and these people were not joking. My interpretation was much simpler; "Get your black butt out of here." I calmly assured Mr. Landlord that I would look for alternative accommodations immediately. After they left, I was beside myself with worry, but realized it would not get me anywhere. Life had become difficult but was not yet unbearable.

It was the last time I took advantage of the corporate intern-housing program. That afternoon, I moved into a local university hostel. I withdrew into myself and tried to focus on completing my internship without further mishap. I stayed broke until a month later when I received my first paycheck. On my way home on Friday, I stopped by the auto parts store to buy a set of tools and motor oil. After lubing the car, I stuck the waste oil containers in a bag and left them in my trunk for proper disposal later. I even allowed myself a couple bottles of beer as reward. Things were definitely looking brighter.

On Monday, I would make my first business trip with my supervisor to visit a manufacturing plant in Tarrytown, New York. Corporate policy reimbursed employees for travel, so I had withdrawn two hundred dollars from the bank for expenses. I was still in high spirits when another college mate asked for a ride from Detroit to the campus where I stayed.

It was the weekend of the formula one Grand Prix races in Detroit, and I thought it would be a good opportunity to check out the cars at the temporary racetrack on Belle Isle. My roommate offered to drive; he had received his driver's license a month earlier and wanted to drive everywhere.

The plan seemed perfect because the beer was making me tipsy. Still, I had a nagging feeling that something was wrong all evening. We drove around the Grand Prix looking for parking and I reached into my pocket to get change for the parking meter. I could not find my wallet! We searched the car, but it was not there. We returned to my college mate's house in Detroit where we had stopped earlier, but it was not there either.

By Sunday morning, I was a bundle of worry. My business trip to New York was the following morning, but I had lost my travel money and credit card along with my wallet. I canceled my credit card and notified the financial agencies about my loss. A paltry $20 was all I could raise from the local Kroger store after writing a grocery check.

On Monday morning, I tried to follow my manager's

directions to the airport, but I missed an exit ramp and found myself in an unfamiliar suburb of Detroit. There was no immediate re-entry onto the expressway, and it took me half an hour to get back en route. There was not enough time to find budget parking at the airport, so I parked in the deck close to the terminal. At $6.50/day, it would leave me $7 after paying for the two days I would be gone. I felt sorry for myself. No matter how hard I tried, something always pushed me right back into the thick of trouble.

Detroit's Metro Airport was packed with morning business commuters and the check-in lines zigzagged all the way to the lobby entrance. I did not know about Gittannes' express check-in and stayed in the line, watching in futile desperation until the digital manifest deleted my flight from the screen. I could not believe I had missed a flight for a trip I had been so excited about. The next flight to Tarrytown was in the early afternoon; I had hours to kill. I tried to notify the office at Gittannes about the situation. For some odd reason, no one was available so I could only leave voice messages.

The small Tarrytown airport bustled with activity when I picked up my bags. Exhausted, I called the Gittanes New York office again, using my travel envelope to take notes as I spoke. Several minutes later, my supervisor burst into the airport with a stoic look on his face. I hastily got my bags and rushed to meet him.

When asked to present reservation documentation at the Tarrytown Hilton, I realized I had left the envelope with my travel information by the phone at the Airport. Without documents or proper identification, my actions looked more suspicious. The confused clerk asked to speak with my supervisor. All I wanted to do was crawl into a ball and vanish from the endless stream of embarrassing situations.

This time, my supervisor did not try to be civil. His cheeks flushed red and his lips were tight. I knew then that there was no way I would reveal that I had lost my return ticket as well. I would rather pay for another one and save myself some embarrassment. But I had no money or identification. Saving my pride was not even an option. I prayed that a Good Samaritan would return my ticket. I rushed to my room and called the airport, but no one had turned in a plane ticket.

I was still contemplating my options when the phone rang. It was my supervisor inviting me to join the group for dinner. I had not eaten all day, so I agreed to meet them in the lobby. I assumed we would be eating fast food just as we did when we ate lunch in Detroit and figured I could manage a dinner burger for five dollars or less. To my dismay, the group had made reservations at a restaurant that specialized in New York style steak and barbecue ribs - mouth-watering delicacies but expensive. I discretely asked if we could stop at a burger joint, but no one would listen. They reminded me that I was on the company's tab and I need not act so cheap. I knew it was time to shut up because the group was already making jokes at my expense.

Dinner was good, but I could not keep my mind off the cost. I prayed it would be less than twenty dollars - it was seventeen. I produced my only twenty-dollar bill and saved face that evening, but I no longer had thirteen dollars to pay for the deck parking at the Detroit Airport.

The following day, I was refreshed and ready to work. My supervisor and I completed our plant visit with no problems. When we returned to the main office, four urgent messages awaited me. There were calls from a Detroit police detective, from Sister Sena, from the Gittannes students' program office, and from the manager of our engineering group. Now everyone at the plant was interested in what kind of trouble I had brought on myself. It was embarrassing. If I had been Caucasian, I would have turned bright red.

Some juveniles had been arrested downtown Detroit that

weekend; my wallet was found on one of them - but the money, credit card, and driver's license were gone. All that was left was my college identification card and a Blockbuster rental card from a store where Sister Sena lived. Since the video card was the only document with a phone number, the detective called the Blockbuster store where he was given Sister Sena's phone number.

The call from the Detroit police sent Sister Sena into panic. She called Gittannes' corporate offices and spoke to the Student Programs coordinator who called my manager. I was supposed to be in New York so what was my wallet doing on a juvenile in downtown Detroit? Had I been robbed or had something worse happened? The panic chain was finally broken when the manager called New York and he was assured that I was fine.

One at a time, I called and explained the whole situation. It took about an hour to set everyone's mind at ease. The detective sounded a little disappointed because I did not know if my pocket had been picked or I had simply dropped the wallet. He could not charge the juveniles, but he told me I could come for my wallet anytime.

With my flight only a few hours away, I called the airport again. No tickets had been returned. As I hang up the phone, I heard my supervisor's voice behind me. "You didn't lose your plane ticket as well did you?" I was too tired and nodded my head to concede my mess. Fortunately, my supervisor knew enough about my weekend to be sympathetic. Once again, he came to the rescue and had another ticket reserved for me.

As the plane took off, I wondered how I would get my car out of the parking deck. Between the chocolate bars and the cola, I had for lunch, all my money was gone. I was thinking so hard about my car that I did not pick up my luggage after we landed in Detroit. Stress was skewing my judgment. I drove to the gated cashier and said, "Do you accept checks?"

When the attendant said yes, I made out the check for thirteen dollars and handed it over. She asked for my driver's license to authenticate the check, and things took a bad turn.

As I explained my situation, the attendant's smile quickly vanished. She thought I was trying to pull a fast one, and I could not blame her. The manager was called to mediate. After twenty minutes of heated discussion, the manager decided to gamble on me because the other drivers behind me were getting impatient. I doubted that they believed me.

Ten minutes from the airport, I realized I had left without my luggage. I could not believe this was happening to me. I drove back to the Airport thinking I dare not park illegally with my kind of luck. Fortunately, a van pulled away from a metered parking space with extra minutes left on the meter. I parked and went to claim my luggage. When I opened the trunk, I was overcome by the strong odor of used motor oil. The oil I had changed on Friday had spilled in my trunk. What were the odds? It was so bizarre that I stopped worrying briefly and broke into laughter. I threw the luggage onto the back seat and spent an hour at the nearest gas station, immersed in therapeutic cleaning.

It took a month for my emotional state to return to normal. I was forgetful for a while but ironically, my antics had little effect on the quality of my work. If anything, it exposed me to many departmental principals who found my escapades entertaining. They got to know me well enough to recognize my potential and invited me to interview for a permanent position after graduation.

Since I now understood dress codes and corporate culture, the interviews were a breeze. My internships had taught me the value of having prior experience before applying for a permanent position. It was unlikely that I could have performed so well if I had come straight from college. Experience had helped to build my professional confidence, my ability to work in teams of talented people, and ultimately, it had secured a job for me after graduation. All in all, dealing with the bumps along the way had been worth the effort.

CHAPTER EIGHT
Corporate America

Three weeks prior to graduation, many students - including some with excellent grades - were still desperately "pounding" their resumes looking for jobs. Most in this situation had no relevant work experience. Even students with marginal grades who had dynamic personalities and significant work experience had a few job offers to choose from. Companies were looking for multi-talented and academically strong students who had been exposed to the corporate world. I was thankful for my opportunity at Gittannes. Without that, I doubted if I would have three job offers, including the one from Gittannes.

A high point in my life, it gave me a sense of personal achievement. Although I had one year of practical training left on my visa, I worried about what I would do when it expired. Time passed so quickly that I was unsure if I could change my immigration status in one short year. Gittannes did not make permanent residency a prerequisite for employment, and I had enjoyed my internships, so I accepted their offer.

Working in the real world was not the same as working as a summer intern. The financial and professional implications shocked me. First, I realized that the job had not brought that much relief from my financial woes. In 1992, I had been offered a competitive annual salary. I had never earned that much money and I thought it was an opportunity to be debt free.

Two months later, I took a good look at my finances and discovered that being single, I was in the forty percent tax bracket for federal, state, social security and the city in which I lived. As a foreigner, I might never be eligible for many federal programs that my tax dollars were used to fund, but I was too glad to have a job to dwell on anything negative.

After taxes, I had $23,000 left to cover my annual living expenditures. I chose an apartment in a quiet suburb, but I paid a premium for the peace and security it offered - $7,800 a year. My old car was falling apart so I traded it in for a new Saturn. Financing insurance and maintenance for my new car was $5,000 annually. Calls to Ghana raised my annual phone bill to $2,400. Even at five dollars per meal and modest use of electricity, my food and utilities were $6,000 a year, bringing my total annual expenditure to $21,200. That left $1,800 or $150/month in discretionary income.

It was worse than I ever envisioned. To afford the three-hundred-dollar suits required for work, I would have to save for two months. I had no furniture and the demands from my extended family made me feel helpless. While I was a student, I could claim poverty, but now that I was working, there was no excuse not to help the folks at home.

How ironic the situation had become. I was afraid to reveal my income to anyone in Ghana because they would not understand the high cost of living. Compared to what doctors made in Ghana, it seemed I was earning a small fortune. I realized that my plight was not very different from when I was in college. I lived in a better apartment, drove a more reliable car, wore nicer clothes, and had a decent job - but that was just about it. I could not pay off my creditors anytime soon, or furnish my apartment, or send money back home. It seemed life in America would still be difficult for a while.

To make matters worse, I faced new problems at work. Now my assignments brought significant responsibilities and greater implications for failure. Though I had patient managers during my internships, my current manager was under so much stress himself that he had little time to break in a new hire. I was confused when he gave me assignments with scant direction on how to carry them out. My new boss was managing so many projects that he probably could not relate to my professional inexperience – he had requested an experienced hire; he did not want to train a novice.

I was the only minority in the engineering department, and I could feel resentment from those who assumed I had landed my position not by merit, but rather because of my race. Others thought they knew the job better and felt their years of service made them more deserving, although they did not have my academic qualifications. I was tested and taunted on every occasion. There were meetings where I was asked questions about the company's product line that only seasoned engineers could answer.

Often, I was cornered into responding with a blank stare. The company produced thousands of parts for several companies; how could a new hire know everything about the design history of those parts? Those who asked the questions had worked on the systems for many years, and it was easy for them to make me the target of their ridicule.

In addition to their superior professional experience, my colleagues were car buffs. They had been rebuilding automobiles from scratch since they were boys. In Ghana, cars were generally too valuable for children to play "fix-it" with them. I was powerless to control the anxiety and insecurity that overwhelmed me, and I needed to be creative about overcoming my handicap.

As time passed my manager began to ignore my memos and progress reports. Once, after I had presented a ten-minute proposal on a component design, he said, "What did you say? I was not listening." I felt helpless. Only the most trivial assignments came my way. I was miserable and dreaded going to work.

The teamwork stressed during my summer internships no longer existed. In the real world, people protected their jobs and were leery about offering help outside their departments - especially when I was perceived as the token minority. The other engineers in the group hardly even acknowledged my daily greetings. I knew what they thought of me. Gittannes was also actively engaged in downsizing and I knew that if it came time to trim the fat in my department, I would be part of the first slice they cut off.

I felt sorry for myself and homesick. I missed being around people who appreciated me. After all my years struggling for an education, I finally had a dream job, only to encounter an obstacle for which my academic training had not prepared me. I needed to talk to someone, but who would understand? The few African Americans I knew had similar troubles. They probably saw me as direct competition – someone who had contributed to their plight. My people in Ghana, had their own issues too. I was loath to unload my problems on them and I prayed for a miracle.

I compared working in the corporate world to being on a basketball team. Regardless of background, each new player had to prove his worth. They might not gain automatic acceptance onto the team - after all, human nature resisted change. My thinking was that even veteran players could get tired or be off their game. If the ball fell into the new player's hands, then the team's success that day would depend on him. That would be when the new player could earn the right to be part of the team.

My day came six months later, when I was accidentally assigned a vital project. A design flaw had been found in a high-performance electronic part. The component was used in many products and a large number had already been sold. Worried manufacturing customers were rejecting new shipments and Gittannes' warranty bill for the part was skyrocketing.

When the project ended up in my department, there was an urgent need for an inexpensive solution. Typically, such a project never went to inexperienced engineers, but the experts were convinced that it would require a radically new design. This would have been cost prohibitive and would take more time than the corporation could afford. The other engineers also knew that the project's high visibility made it akin to committing professional suicide - if things went wrong. They were too smart to be scapegoats. They weaseled out of the project claiming they were overloaded with other critical assignments.

My manager had little choice but to temporarily assign the project to me - the team's weakest member. "Kwesi, do you know anything about micro-processor-based dampening systems?" He asked. I figured this was some trumped-up way to further humiliate me. Why would he ask me about electronics when he knew my college major was mechanical? "I may have a temporary project for you, he said, but this may be more than a fair challenge for you. If you can't handle it, I'll understand."

After the briefing, I knew this project would either make or break me. If I was unable to perform, it would be my last opportunity to work on a significant project and give my manager the ammunition to get rid of me. I even reasoned that my boss might be setting me up so that my poor performance could be used as a bargaining chip to obtain the seasoned help he wanted. I welcomed the opportunity to make the engineering play and vowed that I would do everything to slam-dunk the ball in the basket - anything to set the record straight and make my presence felt.

Although I knew little about electronics, I spent several hours in the company library reading and researching. I was on a mission to save my career. Days passed and I still had not made any headway on the project. Just when a break-through seemed out of reach, an idea came to me. Instead of pursuing new designs, I looked at different industries where similar designs were being used. I knew Gittannes was the industry's undisputed technology leader, and they believed their products were superior, but I was willing to try anything.

I dug until I found an idea I could modify that could be applied to my component without infringing on proprietary work. I thought I had found the solution and was so sure no one had approached the problem this way that, I was counting on impressing my manager with complex analysis.

To my disappointment, my manager was lost in the convolutions of the proposal; he could not follow my model. "Is this not a little too complicated for the purpose we are trying to achieve?" He said. Though deflated, I knew I had been trying to show off. Now, I had failed to sell my idea and did not know what to do next. I had spent more than a week getting nowhere and time was running out. From sheer desperation, I began spending my lunch hours praying for a miracle at a nearby church. In a weak moment, I saw my dreams of a slam-dunk fizzle into thin air. Thoughts of failure frightened me and brought me back to the project with renewed hope.

Convinced that I was on the right track, I began to find ways to simplify the design and make it less costly to manufacture. I seemed possessed by the project as I attacked it with renewed vigor. This time, help came from the most unexpected source. My unrelenting enthusiasm had not gone unnoticed and my manager began to provide me with the resources that I needed to do the job. He introduced me to engineers with expertise in electronics and manufacturing.

Eventually I was able to reconstruct the design so that it was simple to implement. I knew it was time to make another proposal when my main ideas could fit on one page. My manager was so bowled over that he kept saying, "This is a winner, indeed we have a winner!" The subsequent transition went beyond my wildest dreams.

Overnight I had been transformed from a "dead weight" engineer to a "wonder boy." The corporate rumor mill churned at full tilt spreading the discovery across different departments. I began to address several teams and sometimes got standing ovations after presenting my proposal. My busy manager found time to attend every presentation, each time appointing himself the subject matter expert. He always introduced the project as a "winner!"

Finally, I was asked to present to the director of marketing and finance, where we would find out if money would be allocated for the project. Gittannes' finance personnel were the nemesis of creative engineering because they could literally "kill" a project if it did not have a positive effect on profits. Since my solution had the potential of saving the company millions in warranty costs, my presentation went very well. I had purchased a new suit and tie for the occasion and gave my best presentation in the short ten-minute allotment. When the post-presentation discussion took almost an hour

I knew I had my slam-dunk. I was given the green light to proceed, a huge budget, and a team of seasoned engineers to refine the design for implementation.

Within days of my presentation, I was promoted and given a pay raise. I could not believe my success and felt at peace with myself. Now I could look forward to going to work in the morning like a normal person. It seemed once again, that enduring hope had finally paid off.

I never looked back and attacked every project with all the vigor I could muster. Though the petty resentments were not completely eliminated, I had earned my colleagues' respect; I was a part of the corporate team. That was enough for me. Unimpeachable performance had transcended the stifling effects of corporate politics.

CHAPTER NINE
Green Card

My reprieve from earning my stripes at work did not last long. My status as a legal resident in the United States soon became an issue. It seemed that as soon as one problem was dealt with, a much bigger one took its place. Permanent residency or the "green card" granted non-immigrants living in the United States permission to work and symbolized their recognition as productive assets. Although different processes existed for obtaining the document, none was easy. When they could, most foreigners applied through marriage to an American, political asylum, amnesty, or corporate sponsorship.

Marriage was the riskiest way, especially if it was not based on genuine love. Couples had to live together for at least two years and be interviewed by immigration. Within that period, they could become disenchanted with each other - leaving the foreign spouse often at the mercy of their American partner. If the marriage was arranged, there was no legal recourse or public empathy when things went awry and many spouses, including Americans, have had to endure dreadful exploitation of trust and power from their partners.

I had heard many horror stories and vowed to find an alternative means. Kamau's marriage had been arranged such that, he would contribute money every month. When he defaulted for a couple of months, his wife vanished for almost a year. When she was found, Kamau and I tried to talk to her, but she was livid.

As we approached her at the warehouse where she worked, she began cursing at us shaking her head from side to side adding emphasis to each word. "What do you want, and why did you come to my job? You need to leave!" The loud tirade disrupted the other workers who stopped to watch. I saw two security guards approaching, brandishing wicked batons. They told us to leave or be charged with trespassing.

Though we had not uttered a single word, we looked like two criminals. I felt humiliated as I was escorted out of the facility in full view of all the workers. It was sad to be belittled in such a manner, but there was little we could do, no one to complain to, and only ourselves to blame. The marriage was arranged, and Kamau could only retreat in shame.

Even if the marriage was genuine, a green card was not guaranteed. My Ghanaian classmate Lebené, ran into problems after he married his college sweetheart, a graduate student. Soon after their union, they had a child together. But for some inexplicable reason, Lebené's wife refused to provide the paperwork to assist him with his residency status. She decided not to work after graduation and depended on him to support the style of living she wanted. Lebené worked hard, but without a green card he could not earn a decent income.

Eventually, his legal status in the country expired and the couple fell out of love when rising financial problems brought more conflict. It took Lebené two years of begging and pleading for his wife to agree to a divorce. He was slapped with monthly child support payments while he faced deportation because she had sent a report to immigration.

Though the bulk of arranged marriages were horror stories, several genuine ones survived the test of time. I thought those who found soul mates in America were very fortunate; it was not easy to merge two very different cultures. I understood the challenges that the American spouse had to face. There were often too many opposing norms involved. The extended family systems and other cultural links to Africa were avenues for contention.

To apply for political asylum, an alien needed to provide proof of political persecution in their country of origin. This was not an option for me, because I had never been involved in politics. Amnesty was sometimes granted as a political tool to promote relations between governments. In such instances, citizens from the subject country were granted residency status in the United States for goodwill, or when severe political conditions or some environmental disaster had occurred in their country. Ghana had never been the recipient of such a policy.

When someone close to me tried to circumvent the process, it became another horror story. It happened again to my friend Kamau. Though he later developed a serious relationship with his American girlfriend, Kamau still needed a divorce. He had landed a good job in New York, which was to begin after his graduation at the end of the semester. But he needed to produce a work permit in a few months. With little time for anything else, he decided to take a gamble on a questionable amnesty connection.

The program was originally meant for Haitian refugees who faced trying economic and political conditions if they returned to South America. Many had illegally migrated to the Florida coast in open boats under suicidal maritime conditions. But an unscrupulous individual who had connections in the immigration office wanted to profit from the program by offering the same opportunity to other foreigners who could afford his fee.

Through donations from friends, Kamau raised $3000, to pay for the deal. When he returned from Florida, Kamau was in high spirits. Everything had gone smoothly in Miami. He had a temporary resident card that was good for six months - enough time to secure his job for a while. The permanent card would arrive four months later with his new social security card. We were thrilled with the outcome.

A couple of months later, the whole deal came crashing down as we watched, our favorite weekly news program. There was breaking story about Haitian refugees and an immigration connection in Miami, who turned out to be Kamau's connection man. They had a camera trained on him while he tried to make a clumsy get-away in a last ditch effort to elude arrest.

Ordinarily, the program was humorous when the clips focused on fleeing perpetrators. But these issues hit too close to be amusing. My heart dropped as Kamau walked slowly to his room and shut the door. All the money had gone to waste. It took Kamau several years to repair this mess.

The safest method was through corporate sponsorship. Usually, the company would hire talent from colleges or from a foreign country and apply for residency on their behalf. They had to prove that the immigrant had unique qualities necessary for the company's success, and they generally handled all legal costs. I could live with this method and maintain my integrity. It was the reason I had accepted the offer at Gittannes where they had dedicated immigration staff.

As fate would have it, the immigration laws were changed midway through the process. The new laws required companies to solicit more American applicants through postings in internal and national publications, and to justify why they had to be disqualified in favor of the immigrant.

I felt a premonition when my manager and I were summoned into the director's office. They mentioned how highly they regarded my work before breaking the news to me. The corporation could not support my application for legal residency any further. They were not sure they could prove that, compared with other Americans, I was uniquely qualified for my position. I was not entirely surprised since I understood that the burden of proof was next to impossible to satisfy. I still had a year on my interim status before becoming illegal, and I was advised to explore other means of obtaining residency. Failing that, they would have to let me go - "Wonder boy" or not.

I left the director's office still reeling. My manager had surprised me when he put up a spirited fight on my behalf, yet it offered little more than cold comfort. I sat at my desk, overwhelmed with weariness. I felt as though something, or someone was trying to prevent me from getting any reprieve from my stressful life. Nothing came easy. Every inch of progress was earned through exhausting battles.

Barely a week earlier, I had been delving full force into my career. Now I would have the major distraction of securing legal employment status. I looked forward to none of the remaining options, especially since I had less than a year. For all my planning, I seemed in no better shape than my friend Kamau.

I seriously considered returning to Ghana, but I wondered what my life would be. What would I do there? No jobs were waiting for me, and who would pay my bills? It would be unbearable because I would have no money, limited work experience and only a college degree to my name. How would my return reflect on my parents, when they had begged for loans on my behalf? I would be bringing them disgrace if I returned and had to depend on them to live when others had seemingly been so successful.

The only thing left was to marry quickly. Oh, what a predicament, I thought; to come this far and still be so far away from my goals. How in the world would I find an American willing to marry me within a few months? Not an easy task. I had not had a close relation with the opposite sex since I arrived in America, much less, found anyone who would marry me. I never thought I would stoop that low, but I contemplated paying someone to marry me. A few months earlier, I would never have considered such an option. But it looked like the only way out – I had come too far to turn around now.

My mistake was going to a reggae club to find a wife. I walked into the dark and smoky club at around eleven wearing a dark evening suit. If I was looking for a wife, I ought to look my best, I thought. The familiar music of Shaba Ranks thumped loudly through giant speakers. It was the middle of summer, so the girls wore skimpy spandex dresses. The club had a large central dance floor, but limited seating. On busy nights, all one could do was dance or stand around and watch. That was entertainment enough because the reggae beat stimulated dancing creativity; some girls danced with such erotic abandon that I watched mesmerized.

Standing by the dance floor with my bottle of Guinness, I felt I was being watched. As I scanned the club, my eyes locked on a petite, olive-skinned beauty staring at me from the corner of the dance floor. She was dancing alone. She bent her knees and slowly rolled her hips and legs like a butterfly flapping its wings. My eyes stayed glued to her sensual curves. As if to acknowledge my gaze, she turned her back to me and sent her curvaceous body into multiple gyrations.

She was dressed in the shortest black spandex imaginable. As she danced, the dress rode high up her thighs. Her full breasts looked ready to lunge out of her dress. As for her behind, I thought of the song, "My baby got some back." Just like the full-figured beauties in Ghana, this one had some back - and then some more.

When the song ended, I tried to figure out how to approach this beauty, but lost sight of her as she wove through the dark club. Still lost in thought, I felt someone tap my shoulder and turned to find her smiling at me. "Wanna dance?" She asked. She must have sensed that I was a pushover because she walked towards the dance floor without checking to see if I was following. I had taken the bait. She acted as though she did not care whether I danced or not. That was brazen but I was too excited, especially when she danced with her back turned to me. We were so close that our thighs rubbed together.

I could feel myself getting aroused and tried to avoid further contact to save myself from embarrassment. But I was no match this "hoochie mama." I abandoned my feeble attempts to keep my distance. It was hard to believe what was happening to me and hoped that not too many people were watching. Several other couples were dancing the same way - all too busy to give us a second thought.

When the song ended, she signaled she had danced enough and walked off the floor. I followed but before I could say anything, she said, "I want a glass of 'sex on the beach.' Can you get me one?" I eagerly went to order the drinks from the bar. When I returned, I asked her name. She stirred her drink and licked the straw before answering. "Shaunté-Monique," She said.

She had come to the club with her cousin, who was busy with her boyfriend, and she needed a ride home. I was overjoyed because now I could find out where she lived. After the club closed, we stopped for a bite to eat before going to her house. Shaunté asked if I would like to come in for a minute. I nodded my agreement. As far as I knew, this only happened in the movies. My conscience was cautioning me to slow down, but I was like a wild bull in heat. When we entered the house, Shaunté-Monique led me directly to the bedroom.

On my way home, contentment turned into real anxiety. I had just gambled with my life in a game of Russian roulette. The old protection I used had broken and the thought of contracting some disease from this woman made me face the risk I had taken. We had barely talked, so I decided to go by her house the following day to find out more about her; something I should have done before sleeping with her.

I drove through the neighborhood wondering if I was in the right place. The quiet ambiance in the wee hours of the morning had changed into a busy atmosphere. Extra baggy pants and Nike's Air Jordan shoes were the accepted dress code and several walls were covered with graffiti and gang symbols. By the time I stopped by the house, my heart was in my mouth. In the dark, the house had appeared modestly presentable, but now it looked dilapidated. Had the drinks distorted my vision that much?

Several people were sitting outside on their porches, and children were running everywhere. As I got out of the car, I felt nosy eyes following my every move. When I walked up the stairs to Shaunté's door, two young women were sitting on the porch. "Who do you want?" They asked. When I answered, they simply yelled out, "SHAUN-TÉ- MO-NIQUE," and turned their attention back to me. Now the whole neighborhood knew who I had come to see.

Shaunté's neighbors introduced themselves as Sheila and Mika. When I met their children, I wondered how they could live under such conditions. Sheila had three children and Mika had two. Neither of them looked more than twenty, but their young bodies were heavy and stretched out of shape.

The door to Shaunté's apartment flew open and out walked a woman carrying a baby, followed by a man, then three other children. Shaunté was the woman with the baby. Where had my Nubian Queen gone? To make matters worse, the man said, "Are you the one looking for Shaunté?" What do you want? His low drawl sounded like a threat. What a mess, was she married too? I just wanted to disappear. Instead, I said I had just stopped by to say hello on my way home. Shaunté remained behind the man signaling with her hand to her ear. "I'll call you," she mouthed quietly. I wanted to say, "No please don't call." I sped off leaving the bitter experience behind me.

The worst shock for me was the drastic change from Shaunté-Monique, the hoochie mama to Shaunté the ghetto queen. Short black hair replaced the long light brown wig. As for her rough skin, I blamed that on make-up and the dark club. But I could not explain how the full cleavage could look so flat in daylight. Where were all the children yesterday? I sure could not handle a woman with four children.

Though born in America, they were in many ways as disadvantaged as the barefooted village children in Ghana. I felt a tinge of guilt for not giving them money for candy, as I would have done in Ghana. I was reminded of the perils involved in finding a green card woman. I would have to find another way to get legal residency.

But Shaunté refused to let go. All week I tried to ignore her phone calls, but it was impossible to screen calls without missing important ones. Cordial phone conversations had deteriorated into arguments about why I would not visit.

She insisted that the man at the door was her youngest baby's daddy and not her husband. He was just visiting his child when I stopped by.

Each of her children was by a different father. One was deceased, two were unemployed, and a fourth, was in the military. I felt sorry for the children - if only I could give them something without encouraging their mother, I thought. Even so, I was glad for the opportunity to leave town on a two-week trip, hoping this would blow over by the time I returned.

It did not. My answering machine was filled with messages from Shaunté, insisting I had lied about my trip to avoid her. I answered Shaunté's next call and tried to explain. "Where've you been?" She said. When I attempted to speak, she interrupted and told me she was not feeling well. My heart dropped as Shaunté described her bouts with morning sickness and missing her time of the month. That is right, she was pregnant!

I was speechless. How could I go home to my mother with this? What a disgrace! I would be bringing embarrassment to the family that had sacrificed so much to ensure that I had a decent upbringing and the opportunity to come to the United States. I could just see the disgust in my father's eyes. Still, I doubted if Shaunté was telling the truth; it was probably just a ruse to get me to visit.

Seeking closure, I returned to her neighborhood to end the harassment. Shaunté called my bluff and dared me to take her to the pharmacy to get a pregnancy test. No matter how hard I tried, I could not shake the slim possibility that the baby could be mine - if Shaunté was telling the truth. After a few minutes in the bathroom, Shaunté returned with the result - a positive sign in vivid red! My worst fears had come true.

I was scared, confused, and did not know what to do next.

Sensing a switch in the power struggle, Shaunté complained about her ill health and her inability to make the grocery trip that day. She blamed her condition on me, so I went to the grocery store and bought everything from diapers to ground beef – along with some liquor to settle my wayward mind.

Through the next week, my time was Shaunté's time. She complained incessantly about her illness, calling me as soon as I got off work with a list of what she needed. I bought her a new boom box, a new television, and did her groceries. Even her neighbors enjoyed having me around. Often, I brought beer and cigarettes for Sheila and Mika. They were nice people, despite their circumstances

After a week had gone by, Shaunté asked if I was ready for a child. I told her all the reasons why I was not, including being on the verge of deportation. I explained that I could not support the child from Africa. Without financial support, Shaunté grudgingly told me that she would need five hundred dollars to terminate the pregnancy. I withdrew the money with my credit card and gave it to her the following day. Even if things went as planned, I knew I would remain in penance for the rest of my life because of my religious upbringing.

A few days before Shaunté's appointment, my boss scheduled me for a trip to Chicago. I was living on borrowed time at work, so I was not about to weasel out of my assignments. I had never visited Chicago but knew about a distant aunt who had moved there from Ghana. It was important to convince Shaunté that it was a legitimate business trip, so I showed her my travel itinerary. I did not know that she had a photographic memory. She glanced at the travel itinerary and settled down as if she had finally found something she had been looking for.

Upon my return, Shaunté was in a bad mood. She claimed that her brother had been thrown in jail and she had used the money to bail him out. Who was this brother I never heard about before? I collapsed in her living room chair out of frustration and emotional exhaustion. I realized that no matter how accommodating I tried to be, this barracuda would never do what she promised. I was convinced that Shaunté would have the baby. She kept reminding me that we would be murdering our child if she had an abortion. The moral and mental burden was too much for me. I acquiesced and left for my apartment where I could find some peace once I unplugged the phone.

At my apartment, I was surprised to find an urgent message on my answering machine from my distant aunt Esi, who lived in Chicago. Did she know that I had been in town? When I called, her first question was, "Who is Shaunté-Monique?" I was mortified. Shaunté had called the Chicago information and asked for Mr. Asamane. The only number listed under such a unique last name was Esi's, my father's relative. Suspecting that I was married with another family in Chicago, Shaunté called the number and asked for Kwesi Asamane.

Because we were hardly in touch with each other, Aunt Esi thought first about my father, the senior Kwesi Asamane. When Shaunté was told that Mr. Asamane was in Ghana, she asked for the phone number to Ghana. Aunt Esi decided not to give the unfamiliar caller any more information. She had figured that it was the junior Kwesi Asamane who was at the root of all the confusion.

In all my wildest dreams, I did not think I would meet anyone so cunning and mean. Aunt Esi said Shaunté kept calling her house over and over again. I did not have answers to the questions I was being asked. "Who is this woman? What is she to you? Why is she doing this to you? What did you do to her? I felt my life was over now that I had disgraced my family. Though I tried to assure my aunt that I would handle the situation, she was not convinced. She advised me to stay away from foreign women.

I called Shaunté immediately. This time, I was also red-hot mad and demanded to know why she was harassing my family. She stubbornly stuck to her initial conviction that Esi was my wife from Africa, claiming that she knew everything about Africans and polygamy! I hung up the phone and hunched my shoulders in defeat. I was about to have a child by a crazy hoochie mama from the hood. I was too tired to fight anymore; I needed some time to recoup.

I went through the motions of work like a zombie. I was miserable. I tried to work through my voice mail because Shaunté began to call several times every hour. I could lose my job if they knew I had turned off the ringer but talking to this irrational person was too upsetting. By now, I believed that the risk involved equaled the headache I avoided by not talking. Even so, it was not effective for long. Shaunté began asking friends to leave deceptive messages to frustrate me when I returned their calls.

When the calls stopped for about a week, I thought the message had finally gotten through and turned the ringer back on. Then one afternoon, the phone rang at lunchtime, "Mr. Asamane, this is Gittannes security, we have a Miss Shaunté-Monique here to see you about a personnel appointment!" I was jolted right out of the seat - Shaunté at my workplace? I was sure I would lose my job because she was not there to be cordial. My reputation would be irreparably ruined, and I would be fired. Work-place violence had become rampant, and Shaunté could be carrying a weapon to exact irrational justice.

Fortunately, Gittannes security guards were highly trained. The officer wanted to verify Shaunté's claim before giving her directions to my office. When I mentioned that the appointment was fabricated, Shaunté was escorted off the grounds and warned that she would be arrested if she returned.

I no longer knew what the woman wanted. I thought that by agreeing to have the child, Shaunté would become more reasonable but it seemed to have the opposite effect. The situation was bordering on "Fatal Attraction." I had been with this woman once and now I was being held hostage to all her whimsical needs. I had a bad feeling that, just as in the movie, this would not end well. Each time I entered a parking lot, I expected Shaunté to pounce from nowhere.

All I could do was pray for deliverance from God. But did I expect any mercy from God after I had sinned so much? A few days later, Aunt Esi called again. Shaunté was demanding my father's phone number in Ghana to inform him that she was expecting his grandchild. Aunt Esi thought this was serious and informed my parents. Now everyone in my family knew about the whole matter. I could only suffer in silence.

For the first time in my life, I wished I could cry or scream, if it would make me feel better. Things had gone too far, and I could not deal with Shaunté anymore. My mind kept conjuring ingenious images of how I could hurt her. I surprised myself with my horrific thoughts. "Am I going mad as well?" I thought as I realized I was losing control of my wandering mind. I had been pushed past caring. I was fed–up and ready to have it out with Shaunté at any cost.

I arrived at her house amid screeching brakes, the smell of burning rubber, and a cloud of smoke. As I raised my hands to bang at the door, Mika's familiar voice said, "she doesn't live here anymore,' she got kicked out." Shaunté had won again. I did not even know where my tormentor lived any longer.

Shaunté had been evicted because she had started a fight with Sheila and had broken her window. "Why does a guy like you bother with a crazy girl like that anyway?" Sheila asked.

I shook my head and I turned to leave when Mika called me back. She had something to tell me, but she said Shaunté had always prevented us from having a private moment. She asked why I was looking for Shaunté-Monique. When I told them about Shaunté's pregnancy, both girls started laughing their hearts out. Mika was now heavy with her third child, so she sat down to regain her composure. Sheila kept saying, "We've got to tell him, we've just got to tell him!"

Between giggles, Mika assured me that Shaunté was not pregnant. She said if she had known I was so kind, she would never have helped Shaunté with her devious scheme. The urine sample Shaunté used for the test was hers. She had left it in the bathroom while we went to the pharmacy to buy the test kit. Mika was two months pregnant then and needed the fifty dollars she was promised. Mika never received any money. When I mentioned I had given Shaunté five hundred dollars, the girls looked at each other and shook their heads. Shaunté had played me for the money, gifts, and groceries.

Even so, I felt a heavy burden lift off my shoulders. I pulled out my wallet and emptied my money into Mika and Sheila's hands. They did not want it, but I insisted "You have no idea what you've done for me today." My faith in being kind to people had been restored, and for the first time in months, I could see light at the end of a very dark tunnel. Such wickedness could not survive at the expense of well-meaning people.

The next time Shaunté called, I was civil. She had found out that I had spoken to her former neighbors and confessed to masterminding the deception. She claimed she had wanted to get back at me for ignoring her and got carried away by the nice things I had bought for her. As a truce, she offered to take the test again to assure me that she was being truthful.

I watched her take the sample - it was negative. Then I walked out of the bathroom without a second glance. Even

Shaunté knew the charade was over. As I passed the main door, I heard her say; "You could marry me and stay in America." I stopped and turned to stare. Who is this person? Doesn't she give up? Or doesn't she understand that certain things cannot be undone? I had no response, but I thought to myself that I would rather be deported!

Now I had my own horror story. I thanked God that it ended the way it did. I could only blame myself because, for a few moments, I had forgotten who I was, and the basic tenets of my upbringing. I had tried to use someone for my personal gain – and it had almost cost me everything I had worked so hard to achieve.

How could I point a finger at Shaunté-Monique when I was guilty of the same transgression? Although misguided, she was only looking out for herself in a mean and selfish world. What I knew was, to always follow my basic instincts and treat people with respect and kindness. Had it not been for Mika and Sheila, things could have been different. I was reminded of William Shakespeare's poem in the Merchant of Venice, "All that glitters is not gold." My lesson was simple: "Leave the hoochie mamas alone! As for my legal status, I hired a good immigration lawyer. It cost me a small fortune, but it was worth it eventually. With the lawyer's help, I was able to get an extension on my interim status to keep my job at Gittanes. It took a couple years, but we were successful. I finally obtained legal residency in America.

PART III

CHAPTER TEN
Back to Ghana

Sitting at the bar at the Flamingo in Las Vegas, I looked every bit like the corporate yuppie. A blazing red tie accented my crisp Armani suit as I sipped my vodka martini. I had been living in America for nine years and working professionally for four. Gone was naiveté and innocence. Prominent stress lines cutting through my forehead replaced them whenever I was in deep thought. The lines belied maturity and determination, but they also bore trademarks of my difficult past.

I had been sent to represent Gittannes at a technical forum in Las Vegas, a good draw for industry representatives. Most people would have jumped at the opportunity, but I had been to Vegas so many times that it did not excite me anymore, especially since I had no desire to gamble. My job had taken me to many cities in America.

The familiar ding-dong chimes of the slot machines slowly lulled me into thought. I had come a long way in nine years. To go from having no clue about martinis when I waited tables in Illinois to appreciating one said it all. I had legal residence and was well respected in my profession. However, my achievements had not come without a price. My road had often been so rough that there was little energy left to enjoy anything.

Once I thought a good car and a nice stereo were all I needed to be happy, now I had both but rarely the time to enjoy them. I was now a cynical man who preferred his solitude. I did not like what I had become and regretted what life in the States had done to me. It seemed as though I was running away from people because of the difficult situations in my past. The flamboyant Kwesi, the "Mystic Man" Asamane had become a reticent cynic.

Quick passage of time shocked and appalled me. While I was growing up in Ghana, I remembered disparaging talk about those who had been in America for more than ten years - unable to show anything substantial to the folks at home. In my youth, I had naively joined in passing unfair judgment. What was being said about me now? I wondered.

I had not built a house or set up a business in Ghana - the things used to measure success at home. But I felt as though I had ran nine consecutive marathons, each year working as hard as I could without allowing myself much rest. Now I respected those who had succeeded in that sense. Was I doing things the wrong way? It was curiously similar to the frustrations I felt on the track team at Bacchus. Even though I was doing my very best, I was not hitting my mark.

Over the past nine years, I could not believe some of the situations I had survived. Too often, I had been hanging by only a thin thread. I would never have made it without the help of my own good Samaritans. I was immeasurably grateful to the Americans who had selflessly helped me. I was convinced that no matter how many difficult encounters I had, there were always enough Americans who restored my faith in people. I felt I owed these people so much, but I had been so preoccupied with trying to survive that I had not kept in touch as often as I would have wanted.

Keeping up with close friends from Ghana had also been difficult. I had lost contact with most of them. I thought about Togbe, who had been instrumental in leading me through the process of getting to the United States. I had no idea where he was, hopefully, a practicing doctor somewhere. Mawuli, my mentor from Oman Secondary School, was in Washington D.C., where he had completed his Master's in Engineering.

Hafeni and Sheya, my friends at Bacchus, had returned to Namibia after their graduation as they had always planned. Namibia's independence from South Africa in 1990 opened doors to greater opportunities there. With American degrees, they both became high-ranking officials in Namibia's venerated mining industry.

The invisible hand had worked its magic for my Texas friends as well. Kamau worked for an investment-banking firm on Wall Street and had an incredible financial portfolio. He lived in an expensive Manhattan apartment and drove a Mercedes, a long way from his residency woes. After finishing her Master's in Business at Vanderbilt, Akosua Manu, my Ghanaian college friend, was hired by an Australian consulting firm in Sydney. For each, our drive and tenacity had been rewarded.

My mind wandered back to my American family in Illinois, especially my host brother Kelly who had gone to great lengths to make my living conditions bearable. Old man Patrick had passed away earlier that year from cancer. I was glad to have visited with him before he died. I also thought about the two managers at work who had seen that I moved up in the corporation. They were my most faithful advocates. I knew that on several occasions it had taken a lot to fight corporate politics on my behalf.

Though I had done fairly well for myself, I had no true friends who could fully understand my plight. My idealistic views about life in the United States had been replaced by cynicism. Now I believed that everything came at a high price. I envied my peers back in Ghana who had married and settled down with families. I could not help but feel affected by what they had achieved with the little they had. Moose Palla, my controversial classmate at Oman, had very successful business ventures in Ghana. I was proud of him, but it also made me question, my decision to leave Africa. Was my stressful life worth it?

There were several indications that the economic conditions in Ghana were improving. Sustained peace had attracted foreign investors and created an economic boom in many industries. I felt ostracized, like a deserter of an army under siege. Had my departure during crisis, negated my right to stake any claims on the homeland? I longed to be a part of this new momentum and wished I could do something to reverse the uncomfortable alienation.

Homesickness, which had been successfully ignored in the past, now refused to be brushed aside. I often thought about my parents and siblings whom I had not seen in years. I was now twenty-nine and had been gone for almost ten years - too long to be away from home. I remembered all my big plans of going home laden with gifts for everyone and enough money to set up a business. That day seemed more and more elusive. Now was probably the best time, even if I was not completely ready. I went to my hotel room with my mind made up - I was going home. Perhaps reaching into the past would help me face my future.

Returning to Ghana was like an American College homecoming with the ante raised tenfold. Everyone wanted to show evidence of success. Expectations were proportional to the years spent abroad. Sometimes they were so high that it prevented several Ghanaians from ever returning home. It was not until I had prepared a full to-do list that I realized what a monumental task it would be. Airline quotes were financially crippling. My ticket was seventeen hundred dollars, almost all the money I had initially budgeted for the trip.

I still had to shop for gifts. For years, I had ignored most requests from home thinking that, one day I would make enough money to send them anything they asked for. I had received letters seeking my help – from money for food or education to bicycles and gym shoes. They seemed oblivious to my financial circumstances. How could I blame them when I had not told them much about my life in America, and what explanation would I give these people when it seemed I could afford to travel home? I would have to give them something, at least.

For months, I shopped for bargains. I went to flea markets, closeout sales, and retail warehouses looking for good deals. The suitcases began to fill up while my savings plummeted. In the final weeks before the trip, I resorted to credit. I had come too far to change my plans and knew of no other way to make the trip a decent one. I could not live with myself if I did not make an effort to fulfill people's small dreams when they were within my reach. I figured I could always pay my creditors later.

Days before the trip, my excitement was replaced by the anxiety of keeping my finances in order. I was broke, after budgeting money for critical bills such as my rent and utilities. By deferring other bills until I returned, I scraped some cash for the trip. Putting off payments was risky. What if I could not return on time? I thought. Going home had begun as an enjoyable experience, but it was turning into a stressful headache.

The day of my departure, I dressed in casual jeans and a designer summer hat, a habit I had learned in Detroit. I was in very high spirits and ready to go home. Bad weather and re-routed flights made the trip unbelievably long as I struggled in the cramped economy class seats. Thirty-two hours after leaving Detroit, I could finally make out the multi-colored lights of the Accra metropolitan area. All thoughts of fatigue were replaced with euphoria.

Ghana's Kotoka International airport had been completely renovated. I had hoped to catch a glimpse of my family as I deplaned, but it was impossible with the new layout. There were multiple checkpoints and problems I had not anticipated began to surface. Some customs officials were like piranhas joining in a feeding frenzy of extortion. One inspector claimed that I had too many electronic devices; there were four inexpensive portable radios I planned to give away. I was prepared to pay a reasonable tax, but he called out a figure greater than the value of the radios. I wanted to argue but knew it would only make matters worse.

Too exhausted to debate rights with anyone, I handed over the money. These officials wielded enough power to make my short stay in Ghana miserable if they desired. They had confiscated a woman's camcorder when she refused to pay the enormous duty. She threatened to sue, but the officer was oblivious, claiming he would be on vacation for the next month. It was doubtful that she had planned to stay that long.

I resorted to sliding a five-dollar bill into my passport before handing it to the officials. It was like throwing tid-bits to preying fish to distract them long enough to make it safely through their feeding zone. When I was safely through the last checkpoint, I saw my brothers, sister and parents waving wildly at me. I broke into a smile. Just reuniting with my family brought me close to tears. Emotions that had been repressed for several years could run wild. I hugged my family, reveling in our emotional closeness. I felt at peace. Here was one place I could be myself. I was finally home.

Everyone had aged a little and I felt a lump up in my throat when I saw that the years had not been exactly kind to my parents. Although they all looked well, I wished that circumstances had not stolen so many years from us. I hated myself for being away so long. My brothers were grown men. My siblings looked more like my aunts and uncles when I was a boy. At the house, another welcoming party awaited me. It was late Sunday night, but we sat in the living room exchanging anecdotes until I could no longer keep my eyes open.

For the first week, I was bombarded by a constant flow of guests. Though I was aware that many guests were driven by opportunism, I did not mind helping. It was my way of giving back to my family. I would offer them a few dollars, depending on how their "sob story" affected me.

My homecoming was eye opening. No matter how difficult I thought my plight was in America, they had things much tougher. On the surface, the country appeared to be doing well. Gone were the patrolling militia, the roadblocks, and the wary citizens. There was new construction everywhere – roads, bridges, offices, hotels, and schools. But only a few of my old friends and relatives were doing well; many were having difficulty making ends meet. The country's average wage was a few dollars a day, hardly enough to provide three square meals.

The situation squelched any desire for me to explain my challenges or difficulties. I did not want to seem ungrateful for the opportunity I had been given. I empathized with them, while I bore my battle scars internally. My problems were of a different order, and I was not sure they could understand. I listened and offered advice when asked.

I was not aware that other conflicting emotions were simmering within me until I learned about Dela. Our families had always been close and I had been like an older brother to her. Dela was several years younger and beautiful; however, her feisty nature often got her in trouble. When I went to see her, she was pregnant and living in squalid conditions after she had been kicked out by her father.

Her father had so many hopes for her that he was devastated to learn she was pregnant. The implication of having a child without the proper cultural rites was severe. To make matters worse, Dela's boyfriend could not support her at all. He had no dependable means of income and subjected her to all kinds of mental and physical abuse. Even during her pregnancy, he pummeled her with his bare fists whenever she got the better of him in an argument.

Dela's mother wanted to help and promised to take Dela with her to live in Europe. She had removed Dela from the abusive home before discovering her pregnancy. Knowing how much more difficult her daughter's life would be with a child in Europe, she was obliged to renege on her promise. Dela was left stranded with nowhere to go but back to her boyfriend. I thought about Shaunté-Monique and knew how easily I could have been in the same situation. I left Dela with some money and a promise to provide more when I returned to the States. I had seen so many successful single mothers in America that it now seemed absurd to give up on a child for that reason alone.

To discover that I no longer accepted all the traditional views I had grown up with was unsettling. I believed there was still hope for Dela and thought about talking to her father, but that would only be construed as disrespect, since

I could not challenge or disagree with my elders. It was a disheartening realization that dampened the joy of my visit.

I had assumed that my deep longing and love for my family would be enough to prevent clashes, but it was not. Living in America had changed more than just my physical features. My actions were no longer blindly guided by my ethnic culture alone. Now, I could see viewpoints I had garnered from my long stay in America. The arguments I had drawn at home were manifestations of my new psyche. I now had an opinion, which allowed me to disagree freely on many issues.

Such behavior ran contrary to my upbringing and confused me. I had come home in search of answers, but I was discovering new things about myself that I was not entirely prepared to handle. To face the future, my identity crisis had to be resolved, so I decided to visit Oman, where the foundations of my basic character and personality had been formed. Perhaps there, I could re-ignite my fighting spirit and reconcile my new conflicts.

The school looked smaller and older than I remembered - hard times had obviously continued after I left. The tropical climate was the coolest in July, but dense forests made it humid in the Ashanti region where Oman was located. I wiped the sweat from my face and asked the cab driver to pick me up that afternoon, so I could spend the morning walking the campus and taking pictures.

I spoke with some young summer students in the same situation I had been in several years ago. It was as though I could see myself through a crystal ball. I visited my old dorm, and looked for my favorite instructors, who had been a part of what I had become. I left gifts even when they were not available. I recalled the difficult, but wonderful years I spent as the "Mystic Man." Here was where my faith in getting through impossible situations had been nurtured -

the sleepless nights "mining" under streetlights. Adapting to unyielding constraints then had helped me cope with many situations in the present.

Oman had taught me not to accept the country's poor economic conditions as an excuse not to forge ahead. It was the mettle - as my mother called it - that I had acquired from Oman. I was humbled by the comparisons between my situation then and now. I needed to re-evaluate my goals to know where to channel my energies. Where did I see myself in ten years? I thought about my life in America, versus the comparatively uncomplicated life in Ghana, but a decision was not as clear as it was ten years ago.

Now I was confronted with problems I had not faced before. I did not want to argue with my people, but I was no longer the same person. I could not imagine living in America forever, but I could not pack my bags and move back unless I returned with something people could respect. Just like my experience at Gittannes, I would have to earn my way back into the fold. This was not how I envisaged things when I left the country in ambitious fervor. What could I do to reopen the gates of cultural acceptance? I carefully considered different ways to use the skills I had learned in America to do something useful and decided on setting up business in Ghana. I returned to the taxi that afternoon feeling strangely at peace and asked the driver to take me to my old friend Moose Palla. We had agreed to meet at his house for dinner.

The meeting showed me how life could be at home if I was successful. Moose now owned three hardware stores and a house in the most affluent part of Kumasi. A houseman opened the door and ushered me inside. He served me a beer and told me to wait. The ostentatious living room was loaded with the best in home electronics. I looked around, proud and envious at the same time - especially, when Moose joined me with his beautiful wife and two daughters. My friend was relaxed and still full of laughter.

Over dinner, Moose told me that his success was partly due to the improving economic conditions in the country. New investments and construction in Ghana had created a high demand for his building materials. Moose supported my business aspirations but cautioned me about Ghana's unpredictable business cycles. He suggested acting soon if I wanted to enter the local spare parts business before market conditions changed again. This meant that I could not wait until retirement, when I would probably have the time and money to manage the business locally. In America, I had learned to delegate and to operate with expediency, so I assumed that the same strategies could easily be applied to manage a business in Ghana while living abroad.

The remainder of my visit flew by as I spent time with my family. On many nights, I sat trading stories with my mother. She no longer had an income, so I promised to send money regularly to help out. Visitors kept showing up and staking claim to my belongings. They even asked for my shoes and camera. Those were among the most expensive things I had bought for myself, but I did not have the heart to tell them. By the end of my visit, I had given away most of my personal things as well. The whole family saw me off at the airport. I looked at my anxious parents and wondered when I would see them again. My homecoming had been food for my soul. Though I was financially drained, it was hard to leave my family – definitely more difficult than the first time.

I arrived in Detroit with my luggage stuffed with souvenirs for my American friends. I was laden with almost as many gifts as I had carried with me to Ghana. I thought it was an excellent way to express my gratitude to my special people, but immigration in Detroit tested my patience and made me wonder if it was such a good idea. A young immigration officer detained me for hours, and I feared being deported back to Ghana. Were the stories about evidence planting true? I braced myself for the worst as I tried to explain why I went home, and the legitimacy of my documents. The officer did not believe me.

Suspecting that I was carrying contraband, he had my luggage thoroughly searched by special agents. Some of my African artifacts were dismantled because they thought I had hidden something in them. Processed staple food items like gari were opened, searched, and rendered inedible. Then I was personally examined to make sure I carried nothing on me - a humiliating experience. I was at their mercy, and I prayed that they would not plant anything in my luggage or find something I had unknowingly brought with me. Now I wished I had not accepted parcels for friends when I was not sure what was in them.

The uncertain situation turned me into a ball of nerves. I wished I could control my shaking hands and trembling voice. I was sure my nervousness was not helping matters. After three hours, it became obvious that I was not their man, and the officer's supervisor ended the ordeal. I was grateful to be saved from further humiliation and mental torture. Scattered belongings were hastily stuffed into the suitcases. My clothes were wrinkled, and some artifacts had been damaged but I did not even think about arguing.

I hailed a taxi and arrived at home to a welcoming pile of bills. The trip had been exhausting and expensive, but worth it. I had brought with me a renewed sense of purpose and was eager to begin my plans to start a business in Ghana.

CHAPTER ELEVEN
Business in Ghana

Two years passed before I was ready to visit Ghana again – this time for business. I had evaluated the commercial opportunities at home to reassure myself that my original decision to start a business in Ghana was prudent. Renewed growth had opened up many prospects, but I knew that it would be easy to overextend myself if I did not concentrate on my area of expertise. I wanted a self-sustaining business that could provide jobs for people. My experience was in the design, manufacturing, and distribution of automotive components, so I focused on the automotive spare parts industry as Moose had suggested.

It seemed a good idea because in Ghana, vehicles were repaired until spare parts were no longer available. Since scant manufacturing was done in the country, vehicles were imported from all over the globe in many makes and models.

The variety created problems when they broke down. Parts usually had to be imported, making repairs expensive and wait periods lengthy.

A parts manufacturing facility would have been ideal but way out of my financial reach. I settled instead on a small auto parts store, specializing in American parts. I had planned a modest facility and secured business commitments from a few parts suppliers. Armed with youthful ambition, I dove into the project, seldom considering failure.

I needed to find a trustworthy partner with some technical background to manage the business locally. I felt that it would not be fair to ask Moose to be my partner when he had three other businesses to run. My brothers were also engaged in their own business and could not help. Other candidates I had in mind - friends from Oman - had left the country. Forced to look elsewhere, I got into business with Innocent, a smooth talker with technical experience and one of my brother's closest friends.

To finance the project, I asked my bank for a loan of twenty thousand dollars. According to my simple business plan, the funds were to be allocated evenly between capital purchases of inventory and developing the facility. I had heard horror stories from people about failed business attempts in Ghana, but I chose to ignore them. Parts for American cars were rare in Ghana, so I was sure my plan was unique and could not fail.

All the initial planning was done while I was in America. I had invested all my energy and resources to make it work, so I ignored all telltale caution signs and sent Innocent, ten thousand dollars to buy land and construct the facilities. The balance would finance the start-up inventory and marketing. I tried to manage the business with tools I had acquired over my length of stay in America.

Initially I was concerned about depending on Innocent,

but his reports were never late. Every week I received encouraging updates by mail or collect calls from Ghana. Photographs of the small building differed from the original plans, but Innocent said the changes were necessary to save money and meet local building codes. Everything seemed on schedule before I went home for the grand opening.

I had planned my trip to coincide with the completion of the facilities and the arrival of the final shipment of inventory. My family met me at the Airport along with Innocent. Anxious to prepare my business for the grand opening, I wanted to visit the facility the following day. But Innocent insisted that we spend the time at the ports to clear the last batch of equipment. The port's storage facilities were not secure and the longer the goods were left there, the greater their chances of being confiscated or vandalized. Innocent's logic seemed sound.

Getting through customs at the Tema harbor was no joke. First, we had to get in line as early as six in the morning. Second, the customs officials wielded too much power - they sometimes assigned import duty based on subjective assessments. Unlike the petty airport piranhas, these sharks could devour their prey in a single bite. Tidbits were useless; huge chunks of fleshy meat were needed.

The clearing warehouse was packed that morning with traders anxious to get their goods. Others were there to clear their personal effects and cars. Several minutes after nine, the officials arrived sharply dressed in navy blue shirts, black berets, and matching pants. The sun was now beating directly on our heads and creating so much heat that I had to keep mopping sweat from my face with a handkerchief.

We had been waiting for three hours when the older gentleman ahead of me tried to clear his Toyota Land Cruiser – his duty was ten thousand dollars! The man's speech immediately degenerated into crude profanity and derogatory verbiage. "Are you insane? That's why Ghana never progresses." He exclaimed, but it got him nowhere. A smart-mouth in the crowd interrupted his tirade and said, "While you were abroad, did you ever remember to write home?" The man was mortified – it seemed he was the only one who looked surprised about the duty. The frowning officer waved him aside and turned to me.

I had two pieces of equipment valued less than a thousand dollars. The officer took my invoices to the back office to inspect the items. When he returned minutes later, I braced myself for the worst. Even so, I was shocked to learn that I owed fifteen hundred dollars in import duties! How could the duty exceed the value of the goods themselves? I thought. There was an import tax, a luxury tax, a horsepower tax, and a port handling fee totaling fifty percent of an assessed value which included freight and insurance. According to the officer's calculations, the assessed value was more than twice the amount on my invoice.

I stood dumbfounded as the officer waited impatiently for my response. "Master, he said, if you need time to think, step aside. You're not the only one who needs service today!" He beckoned to the next in line. I thought the officer had been unduly insensitive - did he have any idea how long it took to raise fifteen hundred dollars? I knew that those of us who lived outside the country were thought to have too much money, but never imagined we would be treated with such disdain.

All this time, Innocent stood silent and I wondered why. If the goods were confiscated, it would affect him too. I was tempted to let the government have the equipment, but Innocent went back and spoke with the officer privately before we walked to the car. The port official asked us to wait. So, wait we did until four-thirty.

The official – known as "Wicked" hopped into our car

after having a few more words with Innocent. I was too mad to talk so I let Innocent handle things. Wicked wanted a ride home. It took two hours to make a trip that normally took only half because he had to shop first. "Pick me up in the morning and I will have everything ready," he said, when we dropped him off. I was used to more productive workdays in America, but I schooled myself to keep calm. Any argument at that point could unravel the day's work.

The following morning, I was surprised when I entered Wicked's house. His living room was decorated with expensive French furniture and had everything from a micro stereo to a satellite dish. His fringe benefits paid very well. I was even more shocked that Wicked had managed to reduce the duty to three hundred dollars, which included a hundred dollars for his troubles. He had adjusted the assessed value to a more realistic figure. I suspected that this should have been done in the first place, but did not comment. When we returned to the port, Wicked called us to the front of the line to complete the transaction. Such blatant inequity caused a stir among the patrons who had been waiting all morning for service.

After receiving the items, Innocent insisting on sending them to my parents' house. I thought the building had been completed and it would be expedient to send them there instead. It seemed Innocent was avoiding the site. Perhaps he needed time to put things in order, so I agreed to take the equipment home.

The next day, Innocent did not show up. I suspected the worst and drove to the site, hoping there was a logical reason for what was happening. All I could find were empty lots and weeds. After hours of searching, I was tired and upset. There was no facility - for setting up my equipment or storing the inventory. If there was no facility, what had happened to all the shipments of inventory, and where was the money? Only

Innocent could answer those questions. My partner's name was sounding like an oxymoron.

I did not want to burden my family with problems and tried to mask my disappointment by spending more time at home. Although I had told them my visit was for business only, it did not stop visitors from asking for money. They thought if I could start a business, I must be wealthy. Their attitudes changed when I told them I could not help - they did not believe me. My world was falling apart, and for the first time, I wished that I was back in Detroit.

Innocent surfaced a week later. I had woken one morning to find him in the living room with his wife and children. They wanted to have a private discussion with me. I guessed they were gearing up to play on my emotions because Innocent knew that I would not vent my frustrations in front of his family. Apparently, he had deposited the ten thousand dollars in a scam pyramid scheme that promised to double his investment in three months, but the perpetrators absconded. He had done nothing on the project and squandered the money on some bogus deal.

To top it off, he had sold the inventory to pay other debts and his daughter's medical bills. Why had Innocent met me at the airport pretending everything was all right? He could have at least, saved me the expenses for the trip. The photographs, he said, were taken at another project in a different business district. I had heard enough. I walked to the window and stared blankly at the bright sunny day. There was little I could say. I was not sure they were telling me the truth and the betrayal was complete and final. Thank God my parents were not home.

The rest of my stay was difficult. I decided not to seek legal recourse since it was unlikely that I could recover the money - it would only create family feuds. I had to summon enough composure to deal with my family without revealing my inner turmoil. I had nowhere I could be alone to think. I had faced setbacks before, but this hole was so deep that it would take me years to settle the debt. The goals that had seemed so close suddenly seemed miles away.

I left Ghana deeply saddened. Much as I loved my country, I was not sure when I would be back again. Tears filled my eyes as I said goodbye to my parents at the airport. I felt like a gambler who had lost the family savings. I had no business and was in deep financial crisis. I wondered how I would cope once I returned to Detroit – it was a blessing that I still had a job.

A month after I arrived back in the States, I attended a party and met Yaro, an older Ghanaian whose experience helped me deal with my encounter. Yaro had entrusted two hundred thousand dollars - his retirement savings - to his brother-in law to construct a small Hotel in Accra. Two years after the project began; Yaro went to Ghana and found his brother-in-law living as though he had won the lottery. A lavish pool party was in full swing at his newly built terrazzo mansion when Yaro arrived. His brother-in-law had not won the lottery - he had spent the money building a mansion for himself.

Yaro said he tried to get the family to arbitrate, but his brother-in-law had done an excellent job lobbying the elders with expensive gifts. With their authority undermined, the elders went into a tirade about the low wages, suffering, hunger, and how the money he sent had gone to raise the family's standard of living. They praised Yaro for his accomplishment because the wealth had remained in the family.

They even cited one of Yaro's classmates as an example, commending him for buying houses and cars for all his family. Yaro wanted to caution them that his classmate was a notorious drug dealer wanted by the FBI in the States. He had no respectable job and the proceeds from his risky ventures were disproportionate in comparison to Yaro's honest job. Yaro said he wanted to scream at them. "What about me and the sacrifices that I had to make abroad? What about my family? Where would they live when they come back home?" No one could hear his silent screams.

After listening to Yaro, I was surprised that he had not given up. He was planning to make another run at doing business in Ghana. Yaro still believed that Ghana was the best place to settle if he could set up a successful business or make enough money to retire there. He wanted to go home for the very reason why his business had failed – the unrelenting loyalty, of his extended family.

If he was in a crisis, Yaro was sure his family would come to his rescue. The same relatives had bought the plane ticket that brought him to America. Although his brother-in-law had misused the money, he had shared it among the family, which rallied in his support when he was in trouble. Yaro blamed himself for giving them sugarcoated accounts of his life in America – they had assumed he could recoup the money easily.

Regarding his future business dealings in Ghana, Yaro's reasoning was crude but simple. "The poor Ghanaian cannot help anyone when he is hungry, he would have to eat first to restore his energy and work later if there is enough left over." I realized that Innocent may have wanted to do the right thing, but to sate, his material desires, he had gambled away his only opportunity to make something worthwhile in the long term. Yaro cautioned me against judging those at home too harshly since they could not comprehend the true nature of our lives in America. "That is the silent price we pay for having the opportunity to live abroad." he said.

We were celebrating Ghana's independence at the party, where a Ghanaian dignitary was the guest of honor. In his speech, the guest faulted Ghanaians living abroad for not going home more often and encouraged us to invest in projects at home - such irony. I looked around the hall and wondered how many Yaros were present. After our alienating existence as foreigners, it was understandable that re-engaging with our traditional family system was alluring to all of us.

Probably all Ghanaians abroad had their own story about losing money at home. Perhaps the speaker could have asked about our experiences before assuming no one had tried to do what he advocated. That path was well worn and trodden. My situation was not the first, the worst, nor the last.

CHAPTER TWELVE
The Silent Struggle Continues

A year later, I was still buried in bills and disillusioned about the future. I could not plan beyond getting out of debt. All I did was work and think how to make more money. My whole world had become fragile - ready to disintegrate at any moment. If I did not pay my rent on time, I could be evicted from my apartment and still owe money for breaking my lease. My car could be repossessed if I defaulted on the monthly payments, and the bank could garnish my wages if I did not stay current with my loan payments. It would take only one mistake to destroy my credit and make it difficult for me to rent another apartment, buy a car, or obtain another bank loan.

I felt as though I was running down a steep hill with barrels of molten lead gaining on me. There was little margin for error - I had to keep running. The end of the month was the worst because all my money was absorbed into paying bills. There was nothing extra and saving was a luxury. My career was the only thing that I had going for me, and I was fighting to keep it that way.

However, recent changes at work were making me nervous, forcing me to rethink my future. An unusual number of engineers were being laid off, pushed into early retirement, or asked to sign separation papers. Most were seasoned experts with admirable credentials - the only difference was their older age. Whole departments were scratched overnight, and people showed up for work on Monday only to be met by closed doors.

Corporate downsizing was swallowing everyone in its path. Unless I had significantly more to offer, I never forgot who would go first if it came to a choice between an American and me. To stay in engineering was rewarding but rather foolish even though I had a graduate degree in engineering. I had reached a career plateau where most engineers remained until retirement. Trends in my field were moving toward management and it was the engineers with diversified backgrounds who escaped downsizing.

To stay competitive, I needed to have impeccable professional qualifications, so I enrolled part-time at a local university to pursue my graduate studies in business. Three nights a week, I arrived at home past eleven, then I would have to complete my homework before going to bed. It was a lonely existence, but my career was the spiritual fuel I needed to face the days ahead – I had to protect it. In time, I got used to running from corporate projects to schoolwork to house chores.

I still received letters from home, but I had no time to answer most of them. Somebody always wanted or needed something that was beyond my means. Whenever I thought about my youthful ambitions, I would shake my head. How could I have come so far and still be reaching for my goals? I was now past thirty and still fighting the same battles as when I first arrived in the country. How long must I live in limbo?

The double-edged cultural sword had cut deeply. I felt unable to completely meld into the western culture, and ineffective at fitting back into things at home. Like a discordant note on a musical scale, I sounded out of place no matter what melody was played. The lessons I had learned from doing business at home made me cautious about doing anything there. But how far would my career take me?

Sooner or later, I would have to focus my future in one direction. At work, my colleagues had accepted me, but several still bore prejudices I could not change. Social functions were hard on me because our cultural backgrounds were so different. Their fun and games were often not my fun and games and vice versa.

Away from work, there were other challenges. Sometimes when I walked into a store I was still questioned suspiciously as though I had come to rob the shop. Once, a drunken Caucasian called me a rather derogatory name in a mall parking lot without provocation. Just like the African Americans, I was not completely accepted by all Americans. When moving back home seemed to be within my reach, I had shrugged off such incidents as temporary evils I needed to endure. Now that I would have to remain in America for a while, the incidents were not so easy to ignore.

Sometimes, the treatment was so demoralizing that it stayed with me. A year earlier, my Caucasian intern and I went to inspect parts at a corporate supplier's plant. Another Caucasian engineer, who assumed I was the subordinate met us, but addressed his presentation to the intern. He ignored all discrete attempts to correct his error and I remained silent rather than make things awkward for everyone.

When the meeting was over, the engineer said to the intern, "Your man has been pretty quiet, perhaps you might give him the day off on your next visit." A dead silence fell over us because my manager had joined the group at the last moment. After the situation was explained, the engineer turned bright red. He was still apologizing on our way out, but it was too late for damage control. I just wanted to leave. I had heard enough for that day.

Though such incidents were infrequent, some of the perpetrators ranked high on the corporate ladder. I had been asked to organize a design forum for engineers from all over the country. Everything went well until the day of the event, when the auditorium was filled with a few hundred engineers. After welcoming the participants, I handed the agenda to the president of the association - a chairman of another large electronics firm - to present the opening address.

Somehow, the president got entangled after joking about my resemblance to gorillas in Africa. An uncomfortable silence settled on the group. His humor was tasteless. Worried that the incident would escalate, the officers asked the president to retract the statements and offer a public apology. To me, the apology was not necessary since it was not sincere. I understood that I was dispensable, and I would not sue the company only to lose the job that paid my bills.

It was sad that the president's errant remarks reflected the opinions of some co-workers, although they were more subtle. It seemed I needed to prove my worth over and over again. From the experiences of other African Americans, I knew that the wrong response could cost me everything. Still, it was getting more difficult to remain passive about such experiences.

I was also aware that some African Americans were unable to understand African immigrants. If not for my great friendships with many of them, I might have remained in a quandary about how to deal with their hostility. Leroy, Mad Dog, and his fun club, had manifested their latent resentment in different ways. Even years later, an African American store cashier blatantly asked why I had come to America to insult her with six cents. This was after I had asked for change she had forgotten to give me. I wanted to explain to her that where I came from, six cents could have been a child's meal ticket. But I kept silent.

During such moments, I was reminded that I would rather be in Ghana where I did not have to contend with disparaging attitudes from all directions. But the thought of living in Ghana brought forth different challenges. I knew I could not return empty-handed or find employment that would pay a comparable salary. Moreover, I was no longer the person who had left the country over a decade ago. There was enough evidence of my departure from traditional modes of thought.

The expectations of friends and family were high, and I could not go home and ignore their existence. That would isolate me from a warm extended family and make my stay meaningless, if not unbearable. I had spoken to Ghanaians who had tried to do just that but were back in the States within a year, embittered and claiming they would never go home again. They had tried to isolate themselves from their extended family, except it only alienated them further. They had relinquished any claims they had on family warmth and support when they refused to share their good fortune. When their dream projects eventually became difficult to manage, they received no support and returned to America very bitter.

Yaro had not given up because, to him, the alternative of having to spend his latter years outside Ghana was worse than making another try at success. Few had actually made a success of moving home. Some had used their expertise abroad to encourage foreign businesses to invest by offering to be their local project managers. Such joint ventures flourished because they could earn equitable salaries while living at home. Except for the occasional trips to the parent companies abroad, they stayed in Ghana - the best of both worlds.

In my situation, I had many reasons to embrace the homeland. I had to push myself harder, even when every muscle in my body screamed fatigue. I had not bargained on being a prisoner of debt either. I wanted to complete my graduate studies as soon as possible, but how could I pay for additional courses after my business fiasco? There was no room for fun and even going home for a short visit was no longer possible.

Fortunately, there were other things about life in America I did not regret. Long ago, I had confirmed that it was the place where fair opportunity was within anyone's reach. I was impressed with my professional development; my consciousness had been raised while my challenges had brought out the best in me. The invisible hand in America that pushed people to success existed. People still arrived with nothing and became lawyers, doctors, nurses, real estate tycoons - anything they desired.

To live permanently in America was a different question. I was no longer sure the path I had chosen was the right one. All I could say was, "Kwesi, you have made your bed, now lie in it." Coming to America had been rewarding, but recently I wondered whether my professional success was worth it. I felt trapped between two strong winds gusting in opposite directions. On one hand, I was striving to hold onto my cultural heritage. On the other hand, I was trying to deal with the stress that came with living in America.

Thoughts about the deserving ones who had not enjoyed any fruits of their labor and the lesson I learned from Mawuli

- my long-time high school friend and role model - finally put things into perspective. No matter how difficult I thought things were, I realized that I was still better off than most. I had been reunited with my old friend in Detroit shortly after I returned from Ghana. Mawuli had completed a chemical engineering degree in Ghana, and then pursued his Master's in Engineering in Washington. Mawuli's reason for coming to America was to earn enough money to take care of his mother and siblings in Ghana. His family was impoverished, and he was still the only one who could help.

Although our experiences were similar, Mawuli's encounters were more profound. His goal was to build a house for his family so they could live decently. While in school, he worked several jobs. After he moved to Michigan, he still sent every extra cent home to complete the building. I had not seen Mawuli for several months when one weekend, he showed up at my door.

From the troubled look on his face, I could tell that he was in a crisis - Mawuli rarely showed emotion. He had found out that his family had not built the house as he had planned. They had started, but unexpected family crisis had consumed most of the money. Now, they were being evicted with nowhere to go because the new house was not ready — not even close. "What do they want me to do, Mawuli said, build another house? I love my family, but I am so tired."

Mawuli had sacrificed his personal comfort for his family, always placing them first. While he poured his heart out, he posed several questions to no one in particular. "Who would take care of my ailing mother or provide for my siblings if I don't? How can I enjoy steaks when they can't afford a can of tuna? Wouldn't it be a shame if I wore designer clothes while my family in Ghana wore rags? Kwesi, I feel trapped and lost. What am I to do?" I could only sit in quiet sadness. I had no answers.

Mawuli said he wanted children but had postponed marrying his sweetheart. She had grown tired of waiting for him and had married someone else. He had hoped that, after the house was built, he could take care of himself - but not now. He was in emotional pain. I did not know how to help my friend, only glad to be there for him. When we parted ways that evening, Mawuli had decided to live for himself. The family burden was not getting lighter, but he could not spend his life working for them - it would make him bitter if he continued.

The next morning, I woke up to find my front door ajar. Had I forgotten to lock it or had the wind blown it open? It was a bad omen. Later that week, someone from Mawuli's company tried to reach me and left an urgent message for my return call. I figured they were trying to pry into my friend's business, so instead of returning the call, I phoned Mawuli.

When I did not get an answer, I left a lengthy message asking Mawuli to call back. I had not been able to reach Mawuli by phone earlier that week, but he often stayed out of touch for a while. So, thinking Mawuli needed time to sort things out, I waited. When the caller got hold of me the following day, it was to inform me that Mawuli had passed away at his apartment. The police found his body after he had missed work for several days. The coroner said he had died from a heart attack. I plunged into deep sorrow and emotional pain.

Few people knew Mawuli, so there was a poor showing at the funeral home and even fewer people at the cemetery. I felt he deserved a royal procession for his inspirational and courageous life. My friend never had a chance to taste the good life and I wanted to tell the world about this man whose silent struggle through life had been ignored.

Now, Mawuli was no more. His body was so badly decomposed that no viewing was allowed at the funeral home. His casket was to be buried in some public cemetery in Detroit. Even in death, he could not be shipped back home to his family. They would have to dig deep to capture their last memory of the son and brother they had not seen in years. Mawuli's legacy to them was the uncompleted house he had never seen – a life of sacrifice and hardship.

Eyes brimming with tears, I watched as the casket was lowered into the desolate grave. It was a cold winter day. Snow powdering the headstones went unnoticed as it contrasted with everyone's sorrowful mood. Mawuli was only a month short of qualifying for his company's life insurance benefits. I wished there had been money to send his body home. That is what I would want for myself.

It could have been me instead of Mawuli in the casket - all so unfair that I could think of nothing but my friend's hard luck. I remembered Mawuli's prophetic words at our final meeting and it dawned on me that he had left me a powerful legacy. "Do not be in such a hurry to go back home," he said. "You might break yourself in half just trying, if you aren't ready. America is a great country and we can have a wonderful life here if we slow down enough to enjoy the good things it has to offer. Plan for the future, but take it a day at a time. Above all, take good care of yourself, because you are not invincible. You mean more to your family alive than dead."

Three years later, I stood starring at Mawuli's grave again, wishing he could hear me thank him for pointing my life in the right direction. Even with the passage of time, I had not forgotten the depth of his words. I had taken them seriously and resigned myself to living in the United States for a while. A lot had happened since then.

With a mortgage from the bank, I had acquired the proverbial American Dream - I lived in my own home now. For a while, my debts had spun out of control, but I got lucky. New development in my neighborhood had created a considerable rise in home values. In three years, my house was worth almost twice its original value. I had paid off my outstanding debts with equity from the house, and even wired enough money home to make a difference.

Not all my problems were solved, but the future looked manageable and I was at peace with myself. Had he lived, I knew Mawuli would have made it too. He had been so right about his perceptions that I felt life had cheated him again. It was his legacy of advice that saved me.

I understood then that no matter where life took me, I could not give up my dreams. Wherever I lived, it was just as important to take time out for fun, as it was to make a decent life for myself, and my loved ones. Without that balance, I risked losing my cherished dreams. I could stop dwelling on being torn between two countries and accept my new identity as a progressive blend of the two. Instead of being apprehensive about dealing with both cultures, I could embrace the additional roles and welcome the new responsibilities they brought.

If I slowed down and took things in stride, I just might enjoy my life in America and provide something worthwhile for my people at home. Perhaps, that was the elusive element that made the difference between being frustrated in times of hardship and being too emotionally spent to enjoy the good things I had achieved.

The End